Suddenly
He Thinks
He's
a Sunbeam

Adey Grummet is an opera singer more accurately described as 'notorious' than 'famous'. She is passionate about lots of things apart from the colour yellow – her work with contemporary composers and premiering their music, her all-female ensemble The Curate's Egg, making opera as unstuffy and immediate as *Coronation Street*, and John Lewis' haberdashery department (an essential port of call in creating her gorgeous concert gowns). Of course, it goes without saying that at the top of this list sits Fr Kevin Scully, her Beloved. They live in London's East End.

Suddenly
He Thinks
He's
a Sunbeam

Adey Grummet

TRIANGLE

Published in Great Britain in 2000 by
Triangle
Society for Promoting Christian Knowledge
Holy Trinity Church
Marylebone Road
London NW1 4DU

The author and publisher acknowledge with thanks permission
to use an extract from the following:
A Common Prayer, Michael Leunig, Collins Dove, a division of
HarperCollins Publishers (Australia) Pty Ltd, 1990.

British Library Cataloguing-in-Publication Data

A catalogue record for this book is available from the British Library

ISBN 0-281-05244-1

Typeset by Pioneer Associates, Perthshire
Printed in Great Britain by
Caledonian International, Glasgow

CONTENTS

for Kevin
The Beloved

ACKNOWLEDGEMENTS

Many thanks to Michael Leunig for the use of his prayer and Vicky Jenkins for the use of her laptop.

1

ONCE UPON A TIME

I married my leading man.

I can't even offer the excuse that I was young and needed the money because, despite the fact that I was 22 years young, he didn't have much money. He still doesn't but his charms and qualities are those beyond price. I say that in the full indulgence of a love that has, to date, survived 15 years of marriage, several career changes, 14 movings of house, a global migration, Nicorette chewing gum, three moustaches and a couple of beards. I could go on about his endearing idiosyncrasies in quite a comprehensive manner but I will control myself, spare you and fill you in with a potted history.

The Beloved was born and brought up a traditional Irish-Australian Roman Catholic. He ran a mile when, like all of us in the hormone-mazed late teens, he found God to be a ridiculous concept and the Church an outmoded and rather desperate patriarchal attempt to brainwash us all into conformity. In ensuing years he wandered through many ideas, methods, disciplines, combining all of this with studies in philosophy, ethics and comparative religions until he was finally converted to atheism by a man who later became a Buddhist. His combined careers of journalism and acting eventually landed him at my feet spouting Marxist theories in very small cycling shorts. Reader, I was instantly besotted.

He had come to my home town of Adelaide to play the romantic lead in a well-known Australian melodrama, *On*

Our Selection. I was to play the nice girl that the men fought over while being completely upstaged by the comic relief. We spent the rehearsal days running into each other's arms from opposite sides of the stage and the evenings fighting that Socialist Revolution in the pub. He beat up the baddies for me, sang duets with me, moved into my house by opening night and asked me to marry him a week later.

He did this in the middle of dinner. We were having a relaxed sort of meal in a convivial vegetarian restaurant which rejoiced (as did we) in a pleasant vine-covered courtyard and an array of half-bottles of fine vintages. During pudding he had occasion to go off into one of his characteristic diatribes on political analysis and social responsibility. Now, normally I was (and continue to be) quite good at following these through their many thickets but this one – I don't remember if my concentration flagged or it was particularly dense – I reached a stage of incomprehension which led me to stop him and ask him to run that last bit by me again.

'I'm asking you to marry me!' he announced to the entire restaurant in his well-trained actor's voice.

Immediately, and with enormous interest, all diners within earshot put down their cutlery and looked to me for my answer. It was as if I were inhabiting a freeze-frame. I was too stunned even to indulge my visceral urge to run. So I waited the three million years until my ability to speak English returned and then stammered that I couldn't answer him. All the cutlery in the restaurant rather disappointedly returned to its former service and I was left with my heart in my mouth, a hammering in my ears and an unlovely shade of bright red creeping up my cheeks.

The Beloved said that it was all fine and that I didn't need to answer there and then. I could answer anytime. I didn't even need to answer at all. But he wasn't going to ask again – next time I had to ask him.

Now this is all very well and reasonably comical but then the awful questions start. Do I marry him? Ought I marry him? Can I live with him? Can I live without him? Can I live with him and not marry him? Will he live with me if I don't marry him? Can I live without him if he won't live with me when I won't marry him? Do I really believe in getting married? What shall I wear?

A week of this sort of mind-set is enough to drive anyone bananas and my immensely patient flatmate – a gay cellist who did a baked cheesecake that I almost could have married *him* for – was no exception.

When I get worried I wash – not my person but things. I go into domestic frenzies that are exhausting to behold. There is something about pegging out clean washing in a neat line that orders the mind and calms the spirit. I also get vague.

I woke up on a morning not a week after the fateful dinner and did a couple of loads of washing. I hung them out. I had a shower and then did another couple of loads. I made a pot of tea and put it in the fridge. I got the butter out of the fridge and put it on the dinnerplates in the cupboard. I did my flatmate's washing. I had another shower, forgetting I had had the first. I washed the bedspread. I washed my flatmate's bedspread. By the time I had got to taking down the kitchen curtains, he stopped me with a face of desperation and, clutching onto his T-shirt as if I would whip that off to be washed too, he begged,

'Please, please marry him! Anything but this!'

That evening, after The Beloved picked me up from a rehearsal, I plucked up my courage, as well as all visible bits of fluff from the carpet, and asked him to marry me back. He emphatically responded in the affirmative. Then we woke up the poor sleeping cellist and drank an appalling bottle of fizzy wine.

As we had been acquainted by this time approximately six weeks, we thought it prudent to be somewhat covert about our intentions for the time being. The Beloved is the fifth child of seven in his family and all his siblings had done as much marrying as they reasonably could by now. The news that their youngest son was at last planning nuptials caused his parents not much more surprise than the earlier news that he had thrown in a heady career as a hard-hitting journalist to train as an actor. Wearing tights, buying eyeliner, learning to fence and concentrating on his chest resonance was a worry – getting married was normal.

Of my family I am the eldest child and thus I was usually the first of us to do anything. This is a great responsibility. One mustn't write off one's parents' car when learning to drive, or come home a drug addict, or pregnant, or with a criminal record from one's first university party. Then there's a good chance that when one's younger siblings come to it, one's parents can feel comparatively confident and relaxed.

Also this was a delicate time in my family. My mother was turning 50 and was staving off sheer menopausal horror with a huge party. The day after this my younger sister, the last of her babies, was moving interstate to commence her undergraduate studies. It was definitely not the time to announce that I was marrying the opinionated and revolutionary hippy that had inserted his feet under my table just recently.

The inadvertent announcement of our news by a gushing friend, who didn't realize it was a secret, all but ruined the end of the birthday party. I was sent to a particularly distant and chilly corner of Coventry as a result. But the subsequent gentle and tactful and respectful efforts The Beloved made to rebuild this relationship meant that these breaches were eventually mended. And, after the customary months of tearful argument that accompany any wedding plans, and the

uncharacteristic quiet and calm laying-in of crates of champagne and mowing of lawns by my father, we were finally
married in a civil ceremony on a hot summer's day in the
garden of my family's house. True to our alternative convic-
tions, we had no cake, no speeches (except for the moment
my father defied instructions and proposed a Toast to the Bride
and Groom), no bridesmaids, no readings, no telegrams, no
reception line, no Bridal Waltz, no presents, no honeymoon
plans, we wrote our own vows and I made my own dress.

At no time was God mentioned or asked for anything.
The only mild bit of scripture I had timidly proffered was
that chart-busting wedding hit from Paul, 'Though I speak
with the tongues of men and of angels . . .'. This was firmly
rejected by The Beloved in the somewhat steely manner that
I had encountered previously on his exiting from a Christmas
carol service when they read from the Bible. Later when I
pointed out that it was a little difficult to avoid the Bible at
these occasions and wasn't he being just a little bit fussy, he
raved about 'force-feeding' and 'brainwashing', waved his
arms around a couple of times, then apologized and kissed
me tenderly. That always did, and still does, work a treat.

All this besides, at our gloriously sunny garden wedding
we vowed, wept, laughed, ate, drank, sang, and were very merry
indeed. The Beloved and I ended the evening romantically
sitting on the edge of the bath, sipping even more champagne,
with our poor, aching feet soaking in cold water.

And so, dear Reader, began this marriage.

And so it continued as these two performers carved out
their careers, argued with their agents, bought their first
house, worried about their weight, replaced their dining
room floor and bolstered each other's frail artistic egos.

I spent some years in the big Cameron Mackintosh
shows – I was in the original Australian casts of *Cats* and *Les
Miserables*. At the commencement of each of these contracts

was the elation of having made it through the terrifying audition process and the tremendous excitement of spending weeks in rehearsal with the likes of Trevor Nunn, Tony Hatch, Gillian Lynne and Gale Edwards. However this great high is only a proportionally small part of the larger whole which entails a tremendous amount of physical slog and mental discipline. The toll of dancing through injuries, singing through infections, smiling through traumas, tragedies and plain tiredness eight times a week for years is something that should never be underestimated. It was as the glittering appeal of it all was in its final death throes with me that The Beloved noticed an advertisement in one of the theatre newspapers. The musically respected Christ Church Saint Laurence was in need of sopranos for their choir.

The memories of my childhood awash with good choral music and the intellectual benefits of my music degree now dangerously mouldering, combined with the urgings of The Beloved, I applied for an audition. And thus it was that on my one day off singing every week, I ended up singing Evensong in Sydney's bastion of High Church Anglo-Catholicism. I was delighted. I had a musical brain and I discovered it to be still in reasonable working order. I experienced again the heart-stopping mental joys of sight-reading. I sang Bruckner, Mozart, Byrd, Howells, Monteverdi and Stanford, hymns, *faux-bourdons* and plainsong. I sang for reasons other than a pay packet.

The Beloved, ever-lovingly supportive, took to coming along every now and then to see what it was that had so excited and reinvigorated me. And he saw an awful lot in that church that he hadn't seen since before Vatican II. This didn't stem his occasional 'brainwashing and force-feeding' raves. He still hated every inept or bigoted sermon and he always sat near the door in case disgust drove him to flight. But what he slowly acknowledged in himself was that ceremony, ritual, tradition and formality could be a context, and offer a framework for meditation and spiritual reflection, rather than being the stultifying and mystifying obligation it had been to him as a youngster. The very discipline of it all, for such a free-thinker, was an undeniable attraction.

Not long after this we both reached the decision that we wanted to give some pretty Big Life Changes a go. These were a part of growing disillusionment with the government and its right-wing social agenda, a growing personal dissatisfaction in our jobs and a growing disrespect for the workings of the entertainment industry. So we did the thing big, brave grown-ups usually do – we ran away. We ran away to England.

One minute we were everything that bright, young, beautiful people should be, with a lovely mortgage, nice car, insurance policies, the latest in stereo equipment and a positively gripping social life, and the next we were backpacking through Old Blighty in the middle of winter and cashing in our return airline tickets.

This was a blissful state. We had rover tickets to go anywhere on what was British Rail (RIP) and we took great, long journeys accompanied by said backpacks, a packet of crackers, a lump of cheese, a couple of apples and a crossword book. We joyfully spent our hoarded pennies on cups of ghastly BR tea. We sat with our noses glued to the windows at our first sight of snow. We dragged lumpy Youth Hostel mattresses onto the floor so as to ease our backs and sleep in each other's arms. We collected B and B landladies' anecdotes with singular commitment. One day we went from London to Fishguard and back just because we hadn't been on that train before and it was too wet to be outdoors.

When we were in London we avidly haunted museums, churches and exhibitions all day. Every evening we went to the theatre, climbing to the West End gods, craning from the cheapest seats to see things we had been trained to aspire to.

All through these charmed months the one criterion that usually dictated any chosen destination was the presence of a large, and preferably ancient, cathedral. We would arrive at great West Doors, ascertain the hour for the evening service and then slow into a pace of cathedral viewing that would drive any normal person screaming down the nave. Our average wanderings through a monumental pile took us upwards of three and a half hours, reading every notice, information card and guide book, investigating every side-chapel and stairway, walking through every cloister until our eyes ached with wonder and our heads spun with groined pillars, fan vaulting, carved bosses, and flying arches. Amidst Purbeck marble, alabaster and oolite we would repair to the usually excellent cathedral tea-room and squeeze as many cups as we could out of a Pot-of-Earl-Grey-For-Two until the time came to return to the body of the church and perch on a misericord to be washed throughly by Choral Evensong.

Speaking of song, incidentally, I was never going to sing again. Absolutely never. I had had it up to pussy's bow with all that vapid cavorting around on stage. I had thrown my life in the Wait-And-See basket and was giving more than casual airings to thoughts of milking goats and growing chickens and veggies.

This, understandably, was somewhat alarming to The Beloved who was firmly convinced of my integrity as a performer. The woman he married had, by all reports, very nearly been born backstage in a theatre and spent formative infant years parked in assorted dressing rooms lulled by whatever bloodcurdling noises were coming over the tannoy. Her toddler years were spent falling into orchestra pits, choreographing countless sitting-room ballets involving old net curtains and appearing in television commercials. This woman had been a paid performer since the age of three.

One could, with almost immovable conviction, say that the theatre was 'in her blood' – she even calls the postman 'darling' – and now she was going to chuck it in? The Beloved watched and waited with his usual patient indulgence to see with what action I would emerge from my burnt-out state.

Well, I didn't. It took two occurrences to save me from transferring my life from the Wait-And-See basket to the Too-Bloody-Hard basket.

The first was a drunken Saturday evening in Edinburgh. That is, not simply the beneficial effect of one of these in itself, but what happened during one of them. More accurately I should say it was what I don't remember happening that was the turning point. It seems that, in the company of some old friends from Australia that were now resident in that fair city, I agreed to sing with them in their church choir the following morning. That Sunday morning found me, having not sung a note or even had a bit of a warble in the bath for six months, nursing a hangover that seemed to colour all things pus-green and puce, sight-reading my way through the service in St Cuthbert's Church below the famed castle.

The things this woke in me, apart from a renewed determination never to drink again, were more than I could ignore with any honesty. The thought that I might be very wrong to deny talents that I so obviously had gave me a few resounding blows in between those of my cranial jackhammer. And the important, simple and terribly difficult fact to remember as a singer is just how much pleasure singing brings to people. I was trained to do it and I was good at it – what was it I was so resolutely avoiding?

The second occurrence was a good old, down-home style heart to heart with The Beloved in a godforsaken pub in Swansea. He took me firmly by the shoulders, fixed me with an unflinching regard and said, 'So what are you going to *do* with your life, Adey?'

As conversational gambits go, this was a doozy. I responded, with all my anguish and soul-searching boiling over, by bursting into tears. Then I decided, then and there, to move to London, find a singing teacher and start singing real, hard-core classical stuff. No Lloyd Webber allowed, not even Sondheim – we were being serious and grown-up now and giving it a serious and grown-up go. The main reason for making such a lightning resolve was not that I had over-much confidence in my abilities at the time but that I suddenly felt it would be more than horrific if I looked back from a disappointed age of 70 and had never given it a whirl.

So there you have quite a few of my Life Changing Moments all before Chapter 2. The LCM that I have omitted till now though was not mine – it was The Beloved's.

Having left Sydney with several recommendations as to where to find good choral music in London and having kept up a reasonably regular Sunday attendance at services in all our travels, we decided on St Bride's Fleet Street as the spot for Midnight Mass on Christmas Eve. We arrived in loads of time, were greeted warmly by the Rector, were advised to play German Beachtowels on the front-row seats with our coats and to wander in the immensely interesting crypt until time.

The service began with the usual throat-clutching solo of *Once in Royal David's City* and as we thundered in at the second verse and the choir processed to their stalls, I noticed with a smile that the lead soprano was heavily pregnant. The glorious singing continued through the liturgy until the invitation to Communion, when we usually sat down quietly and respectfully. But The Beloved stood up again, hesitated pinkly and then, with a straight back and his blue Irish eyes intent, joined the queue to the altar.

I stared.

I thought, 'I think I'm shocked!' and then I thought,

'No, perhaps I'm not. Perhaps I've smelt this coming for a while', and I waited to see what would happen next.

What happened next was nothing to do with the roof opening and crowds of angels appearing or shafts of light falling upon him. What actually happened next was that the pregnant soprano extricated herself from the choirstalls and waddled out of the church in a hurry. Was she in labour? Was it now? A Christmas baby? As no one else moved, none of her colleagues raced to her aid and no sirens or alarms sounded, I eventually concluded that things must be under control. The service ended just as it should have with *Hark the Herald*. The choir was, though, one soprano down now so during the procession out, the countertenor who had stood next to her, to my colonial astonishment, burst into the descant of the last verse at a volume four times as loud as the remaining sopranos combined.

Of these three unusual incidents that evening, I don't know which actually surprised me more, but I am quite certain of which had the most lasting personal impact. I hope I don't disappoint Andrew (the countertenor) too much when I say that it was not his singing.

2

FIRST AID

I am sure I don't need to overemphasize the fact that the Church of England is a formidable institution.

Were I to be slightly paranoid, I could live under the impression that there is simply no getting away from it and its agents are absolutely everywhere. These days I try not to be at all surprised when every set of theatrical digs I turn up in happens to be run by a church warden, organist, clergy off-spring or parish secretary. Within 24 hours of my arrival, the local vicar will have happened to be popping in and we will all realize that all the people we have ever known in our entire lives were at school together. I am at a loss to explain this phenomenon apart from the half-spooky, half-reassuring thought that there really is someone up there looking out for me.

On my departure from Christ Church Saint Laurence in Sydney, the Director of Music had been so kind as to give me a few letters of introduction to musicians in London churches and to provide me with a few morsels of useful low-down. Once I had grasped the nettle in the Welsh pub and decided to give the classical singing lark a go, I contacted these people and was promptly whizzed into an audition by two of them. Equally rapidly I found myself in the vastness of St Alban's Holborn giving voice from the west gallery while an absent regular member dealt with the after-effects of a car crash. A little while later I was offered a regular position myself at that bastion of high-church theatricality, that shrine of Anglo-Catholicism, that architectural splendour, All Saints, Margaret Street in W1.

Through all this The Beloved continued to manifest occasional, but not yet alarming, symptoms of what we now know was to become a galloping condition. One could say that he was, as yet, at a slow walk and had not yet even broken into a trot, never mind a canter. Almost unobtrusively, the word 'prayer' replaced 'meditation' in his lexicon. He would, every now and then, take himself off to weekday Choral Evensong at cathedrals – just to hear the singing, you understand. He would suddenly plunge downward in genuflection while we were wandering around chunks of historical church architecture. He usually came along to church wherever I was singing and expressed more than once, or even more than twice, a sprouting interest in the form of service. He actually listened to sermons and, this was really weird, could discuss their finer points afterwards in the pub.

Now you'll be thinking, 'Sure, it looks like he's got a touch of the church bug but it's nothing serious, nothing to worry about.' And that's what I thought too, dear Reader. I thought it would all settle into a normal, reasonable English type of churchgoing after the initial infection. After all, it was not as if he had had any blinding conversions, nor had anyone beetling around in a cloud or a pillar of fire spoken portentously to him. Everything would calm down, the patina would fade, the hurricane would pass and he would get on with being a normal, tortured, angst-ridden, impoverished writer. Snafu. It was like he was undergoing an inoculation – he'd get a mild fever for a while and then be immune. Little did I know that this virus was more enduring and insidious than herpes or malaria. Once caught, they make themselves comfy in your spinal cord for the rest of your life, but this one lives in the heart and soul.

One of the first incidents that did cause the alarm bells to give a little tinkle occurred in St Alban's Holborn. I was perched miles above the earth in the aforementioned west gallery and letting a few decibels loose for the processional hymn. The occasion, I seem to remember, was a feast of the Virgin Mary, that of her bodily Assumption into Heaven.

Of all the wonderful and bizarre myths that have grown up around the person of the Blessed Virgin Mary, this is one of the few that has actually got so far as to be declared an actual fact by an actual Pope, the twelfth chap to be called Pius to be precise. So convinced was he by the overwhelming force of 15 centuries of observance and belief that he did this in 1950. He declared that so very blessed was the Blessed Virgin Mary that Divine Will just couldn't let her suffer mortal corruption and decay. So things were sorted so that she would be assumed bodily, fast asleep if the doctrine of the Dormition is to be believed as well, into Heaven. One surmises that if she was asleep, she woke up a bit later because there she is to this day, a constant and sympathetic listener to all our woes and difficulties.

I could get all earnest about the Gaia/Earth Mother/ Goddess correlations and make a lot of eye-contact about right-brain, feminine and intuitive psyche and lunar cycles but I won't. I will simply state that I have developed a great personal devotion to Our Lady whose myths, properties and nature I have absolutely no need to prove.

Imagine my surprise, kind Reader, when, in the midst of verse three of this hymn, my attention was drawn downward by a colleague to the enormous, lace-draped, flower-festooned statue of the Blessed Virgin Mary being carried at shoulder height in procession around the church. Small girls in blue sashes were tossing petals before the sanctuary party, highly starched acolytes in deep lace solemnly paced in ranks, incense was wafting upwards in clouds and through this I discerned the top of a familiar head. The Beloved was one of the four strapping men bearing the litter with the statue teetering atop it. And, in a clever piece of organization, each of these fellows chosen was of a different height so it was that Our Lady rolled and lurched her way around the aisles a couple of times before swaying her way up the nave to the sanctuary. The hymn rumbled and roared on through verses four to seven with one soprano voice temporarily missing.

This was the sort of small incident that became more and more frequent. When I took up the post at All Saints, The Beloved became my regular companion. My duties of a Sunday encompassed rehearsing and singing the morning Mass, drinking a measure or two of gin in the church bar in the crypt, repairing to the pub when the bar closed, then returning to church again to rehearse and sing Evensong and Benediction and then doing the bar and pub bit all over again.

At the time we were living with a friend in the leafy propriety and niceness of Cheam. Being rather closely strapped for cash, we couldn't afford the fares to go home there for lunch between services. Neither, sadly, could we pay our way if we joined the other choristers in the week's chosen restaurant more than occasionally. While the summer weather lasted we took to packing sandwiches and having picnics. However this practice wistfully faltered under the vagaries of the English autumn until we discovered that the Victoria and Albert Museum (entry to which was then still free to its owners, the people of the British Nation) has a lunch room. This was usually used for confining the sour-smelling chaos of visiting school parties while they wolfed bags of unlikely and nutritionless snacks, employed their sandwiches as lethal missiles and left the tables stickily puddled with highly coloured liquid described on the containers as 'drink'. But on a Sunday it was completely unoccupied territory.

We would, after we had firmly restrained ourselves from throwing our own sandwiches at each other and eaten them instead, choose a particular gallery to concentrate on from the floor plan. Then we would march briskly through the mazes of other galleries, shielding our eyes and muttering, 'Don't look. Don't look' to each other until we reached our goal. We simply had to be this purposeful or we would never have made it past the myriad of fascinating and compelling exhibits that we had decided to forgo on that visit. Once, on a particularly cold and miserable Sunday, we found ourselves too tired to wander through a single one of the wonderland galleries. However we hit upon the plan of repairing to two unobserved seats that we knew of on one floor. There were heating grills under these as well and the room was out of the way of the usual route of tourists. With ornate casualness we took up occupation and remained blissfully cosy and undisturbed for an hour and a quarter's nap.

We also varied our culturally explorative diet with visits to the Museum of London, the only other museum open when we needed it. Sunday by Sunday we worked our way chronologically through this fair city's impressively displayed history, picking up each time, methodical bunnies that we are, where we had left off the time before. The Beloved's favourite display here was the darkened room in which was the Great Fire of London exhibit. The actor's recorded voice-over so thrillingly announced, 'And then, . . . disaster!' that we returned regularly to gasp at the light-show flames licking realistically up the walls and to shiver at the portent of the script.

But back to All Saints.

To me, in my trial run there, all the other choristers were terrifyingly competent. They gave off the cool air that either they had sung a piece so often they could do it in a coma, or that their sight-reading was so unfailingly accurate that it sounded like it. There were 'in' witticisms about the music or other choirs. It was assumed that one knew every nuance of liturgy and was conversant in Latin. One gentleman, who shall be nameless, spent the entire rehearsal caringly and supportively tsk-ing and groaning behind me at every wrong note I sang. The women of the choir were afterwards herded into a separate room off one of the various subterranean passages under Margaret Street where we donned extraordinary robes and made coffee to serve to the men. Our demeanour, once upstairs in church, was rigidly prescribed and I was instructed in the arts of turning hospital corners in procession and remaining perfectly in step with my partner and of holding my hands at rib height, the right hand uppermost with its fingers curled in the palm of the left. This position was to be assumed whenever we were standing without music in our hands. We were to genuflect in military chorus to a curt signal from the cantor and, although we were permitted to show interest in the preacher, we were never to look at the congregation.

I left the church after that trial run in the sure and fervent hope that I wouldn't get the job.

I got the job. I was placed in the choir stalls in the position that Laurence Olivier occupied when a choirboy there and recommended my journey through the boundless glories of church choral music. I must, in fairness to the place and its denizens, say that the rigidity did lose its terror for me as the traditions and observances of the place became more familiar. Over the years it has also relaxed considerably to a point where the choir now has an air of dignified poise rather than army precision. And the men make their own rotten coffee.

The really exciting thing about this appointment was that The Beloved and I, with no family in the UK and only a few friends, abruptly seemed to have landed in the midst of an entire community and included without demurral or question. Well, actually there were a few questions about The Beloved's shoulder-length hair, about why we had left a country that had such an abundance of fine weather and about what was happening in *Neighbours*. Our mild Australian accents were also imitated tirelessly to a point where, in an admittedly bad-tempered outburst, I accused a dear colleague of racism. Apologies were proffered all round, but I still maintain that if I were granted a fiver every time some Brit, in a scintillating exhibition of his facility with dialects, regales me with 'Geed-eye myte!' I would not today be travelling economy class.

A couple of months on a very steep learning curve brought me to a proud moment. I was taken gently aside by the Director of Music and, just as I thought I was about to be spoken to about laughing too much or the plethora of my wrong notes, he asked me to sing my first solo. A couple of weeks later, with The Beloved clenching himself in anticipation in the congregation, I trembled my way through *Laudate Dominum* from Mozart's *Vespers*. As the last chords died away, and before I could finally buckle in relief, a woman stood up in the midst of the congregation. My immediate panic-stricken thought was that the Music Police had finally caught up with me for mauling Mozart.

What she actually did was to order the whole congregation to rise up and walk from this idolatrous temple of Mammon and follow her to her church nearby where 'real, scripturally-based' worship was enacted and we were led to understand that the Holy Spirit whizzed about the place somewhat like a released balloon and they all held their hands in the air to catch it. Needless to say she was ever-so-politely ignored and the sides-people quietly posted her out of the door.

So how was The Beloved's infection going by this time? Well, as at Christ Church Saint Laurence, the liturgy was like nothing he had seen since his Irish-Catholic childhood, so there was something of a deep-seated connection to such formality and measure. However, what had been normal and part of what everybody did every day to a young, working-class stripling was here enhanced and heightened in a way that could only appeal to his innate theatricality. That is not to say that it was all ponce and no substance. Far from it. Here, amid the excesses of the West End, was a calm and contemplative centre, a place of extraordinary beauty, an oasis of peace. Here was a house of prayer.

After a few months of regularly occupying a pew at All Saints, The Beloved was approached by the Vicar and asked if he fancied becoming a server. To this he readily agreed, being the sort of chap that believes in getting involved and doing his bit towards keeping things running. He was accordingly allotted a cassock in another of the subterranean hidey-holes and was painstakingly trained by the remarkable Cedric, a gentleman of boundless pacific tact and iron will. I will say that never had All Saints seen quite such a long ponytail on an acolyte, nor had they experienced the occasional expletives The Beloved was given to muttering in the sanctuary. While both of these were the subject of much sibilance in the bar, there was not much eyelid-batting in church and we both felt very much part of the furniture and supported as we struggled to put down roots.

On the home front, we had now found our own little flat in South London and had sold my car, rather than our bodies, in order to pay the rent for a while. The bulk of our bijou income was made up by the backstage and wardrobe work we both had fallen into under the rapier-witted patronage of Katie, head of the costume department at the Royal National Theatre. This earthy and wry saint kept us both bobbing above the poverty line for years and has since been fittingly immortalized in one of The Beloved's plays.

So there, I have laid out the *mise en scène* for our drama to play in. We had an address, telephone number, bank accounts and National Insurance numbers. We had friends to have dinner with. We had workmates to have a drink with. We undoubtedly lived somewhere after all the months of nomadism.

When friends or colleagues ask me, 'So what really did happen?' I find it more than a little bit of a test to reply in less than 300 words. I like to assume that I am being asked for a reason, however casual the enquiry, and so I try to answer with clarity and honesty. It goes something like this:

Our move from Oz to London brought The Beloved, with the experience of all his explorations, into proximity with a good millennium or so of church tradition. He started to see his own discoveries and insights from the view-point of historical language and ancient practice. He could call the new things by old names. Or vice versa. Or both. He could feel that the history was a support to spirituality and a vast resource instead of a millstone. And I think it was terribly, terribly brave of him to move so openly and inquisitively into this territory.

There you go – 97 words.

3

INTENSIVE CARE

Of course, all this meant that breakfast-table conversation in the South London flat changed markedly. As did dinner conversation, the conversation over cups of tea, the conversation over bottles of the really-quite-drinkable local Vino Desperado and the bedtime conversation after lights out. The change was not so much in form, but content.

The Beloved has always been given to rehearsing passionately held views to willing listeners. The occasional raves that had led us skipping through philosophy, language, art and leftist politics now changed to something that dragged me by the hair through ideas and concepts I had no vocabulary to deal in. Your average music degree doesn't dwell over-much in eidetic reduction, phenomenology or exegesis. I wanted so desperately to be a useful sounding-board for him but I simply didn't speak the language.

This was the first letting go.

There were to be many, many more of these, each just as painful and as inevitable as the last. This first one hit me like an avalanche. I had to wake up to the idea that our relationship was no longer a self-sufficient intellectual and spiritual world. The Beloved seemed to be disappearing from my sight into new territory where I could not follow. I might have insisted that he carry me too, that he tuck me into some sort of philosophical side-car, but I knew that this would not be right or truthful. I had to permit him to go.

I don't believe that he saw this dilemma in quite the fearsome way that I did. I was, quite simply, frightened for my marriage. The way it had been until now was intangibly no longer viable and I was at a loss to know how to do it any other way. But I also recognized honest conviction when I saw it.

While The Beloved was away trolling around Europe playing Jimmy Porter in a wincingly under-rehearsed production of *Look Back in Anger*, I summoned my courage from wherever it normally lives and took these fears and confusions to a sympathetic mate. Fr Simon was the curate at All Saints and what fiction usually describes as 'a thoroughly down-to-earth Yorkshireman'. I figured if anyone could explain all this in words of one syllable, he could. And I was right. He put down his pint, sucked his top lip and said, 'Ooh, I think it's time he came to see me.'

Desperately grateful to have passed whatever the buck was, I informed The Beloved the moment of his return, with only the merest trace of hysteria in my voice, that he had an appointment with Fr Simon next Tuesday and that was that.

The Beloved had the vestigial energy to look a bit shocked through the grey of the exhaustion borne of nearly a month of one-night stands of the theatrical sort. Each night they alternated between *Look Back* and *As You Like It*, playing a different town every two days. In the long-held and long-hated tradition of small-scale touring, the actors were their own crew so they themselves drove the bus full of actors and the truck full of borrowed and home-made scenery around the mysteries of Belgian motorway exits and Dutch one-way systems to each new venue. They would then unpack everything, build the set, build the lighting rig, focus all the lighting, rehearse anything that went wrong last time, don the equally borrowed and home-made costumes, give telling and intense performances of these two milestones in the British dramatic *œuvre*, take the costumes off again, down a brisk pint, dismantle the lighting rig and set, repack the truck and try to find a hot meal in town at midnight. Isn't an actor's life glamorous and exciting?

While enduring the hisses of feministic German women for his portrayal of the beastly Jimmy Porter, he did derive a small measure of delight from being able to speak the word 'pusillanimous' several times a week. In the Shakespeare The Beloved played both the wicked Duke (complete with black swirly cloak and moustache) and Sylvio, the simple, lovelorn shepherd lad and comic relief. Well, he is usually played as comic relief but in this production, which (for a no doubt deeply artistic reason) was set in eighteenth-century Spain, the director had decided against the convention of playing Sylvio for laughs. The Beloved was directed as serious and desperate. Then he was given, for a costume, a knee-length poncho and a four-foot wide sombrero. This milliner's triumph was too large to be adequately stiffened so audiences, probably slightly mixed up about the number of Spaniards wandering around the forest of Arden anyway, were even further confused by the sight of The Beloved's Sylvio hurtling onto stage, pleading, 'Sweet Phoebe! Spurn me not!' barely visible underneath this mighty sombrero which continued to undulate around his shoulders for minutes after he had reached a standstill. Every time he moved the straw would break into its wave-like motion again. Not surprisingly, he was absolutely hilarious.

This poor, hard-working actor crawled up the stairs to his sweet home only to be greeted by his loving spouse commanding him, before he had even opened the pungent riskiness of his dirty washing bag, to go and discuss spirituality with a priest.

In all the years of our marriage to date, I am still daily assured of his passionate regard and tender indulgence of me.

On this occasion, having recovered from his initial, weary surprise, he simply agreed. The appointment was met and Simon became The Beloved's first spiritual director.

The first thing this seemed to involve was a lot of books with 'God' and 'Me' written on the front with pictures of sunsets and daisies coming into the house. I hated this. I felt hot embarrassment when visitors spied any lying around the sitting room that I had failed to hide away before their arrival. I curtly dismissed any timid suggestion from The Beloved that I might actually read one. I cringed when he brought one out to read on the Underground, convinced that our fellow passengers were sniggering or whispering behind their hands.

I suppose anyone with any passing acquaintance with Elisabeth Kübler-Ross would point out that I was in full-scale denial. They would be right. If there was a panic button I had smashed the glass and was sitting on the damn thing.

This state of palpitation was also complicated by the fact that, while The Beloved was in Europe, my mother in Oz had been diagnosed with breast cancer and, very soon after, underwent a radical mastectomy.

She wouldn't let me go to her. Her reasons were that she was surrounded with friends all supporting her like mad, she was not actually dying yet and she badly wanted quite a bit of time on her own. First, to deal with the great shock of the diagnosis, but also to try to assimilate the tremendous amount of advice she was given while in this shocked state. From the wealth of this medical, alternative and experiential advice, she then had to make important decisions about how she wanted to direct her surgery and the ensuing treatment. Being a trained pharmacist herself she was well-versed in the medical possibilities and she decided to supplement her chemotherapy with a combination of vitamins and an organic vegetable diet. Actually, she decided all that after she had had a go at treating the mutant cells herself with a good quart of neat brandy every day hoping she might 'pickle the bastards'. She said she didn't feel she really needed me there yet and she promised to be honest about when she did.

I am inordinately proud to say that she survived, has had her boobs rebuilt and has been clear of cancer for eight years. At the time of writing, having finally retired from her pharmacy career and her concurrent one as a textile artist, she has retrained in photography and electronic imaging and won an award for one of the highest matriculation results in the state. She is also designing and building her own ecological and energy-efficient house. I very much hope that when I grow up I'll be like her.

Meanwhile back in South London, storms all blew themselves out and, while I still found the God books deeply alarming, The Beloved was happily industrious and absorbed as he read and discussed and read and discussed and so forth. My panic subsided to some extent as I simply got used to these changes. A life in theatre is a good, if faintly exhausting, training in the art of moving on. People one is working with today will be best-friends-for-the-rest-of-one's-life for three weeks. Then, once the gig is over, everyone exchanges phone numbers and makes promises of lunch, which everyone also knows will never be kept, and disappears from one's life. There is nothing wrong or culpable in this, it is simply life in the theatre. No one means anything nasty by it, it is just a mistake to take it seriously and you can make yourself good and miserable if you do. The ones who do ring and do have lunch, they're the ones to treasure. They are the jewels of friends who know what you look like dripping with sweat in a corset and wig and they'll still take you out for a drink.

The Beloved, while never excluding me from the process, was really quite shy about what was going on between him and Simon. Or perhaps I should say between him and God with Simon acting as some sort of diplomatic interpreter. I never really knew what they discussed or did, and when I did attempt to pry a little, The Beloved would gently deflect me or apologetically tell me that it was a bit sensitive and private. He once told me that he felt he was catching glimpses of some reflection in a still pool but every time he tried to touch or hold on to what he perceived, he destroyed the vision. He also said that it was very much like an itch and you know what happens once you start scratching.

The Beloved was doing all this exploration with the singular commitment and honesty that he brings to everything he undertakes. He even washes up with a minimal amount of washing-up liquid out of consideration for the environment. He shops for those products with the least packaging and he re-uses envelopes. He lobbies for better public transport, he meets deadlines, he refuses to have a mobile phone and he wears only natural fabrics. There is no television in the house. He does all this and more with unflagging energy, not because he feels superior or even holier-than-thou, but because he passionately believes that it is right to do so and that we should do what is right. The good intentions and resolutions that the rest of us make with flash-in-the-pan conviction on the first of January, he keeps and doesn't falter. It's utterly admirable and dead spooky.

By no means, though, do I wish to make him out as a paragon. Just to balance the scales, he has an explosive temper, a furtive weakness for chocolate, a delight in tickling me which I hate, a scatological leaning in his humour, a pernickety obsession with punctuality and illegible handwriting.

This light of my life, this best friend and lover, this great-hearted clown came home to me one grey February day with a serious look. He had been to see Simon that morning and, with a purposeful line to his genetically inherited chin and a catch in his voice, he blurted, 'I think I've got to do it.'

My reply was just as yours, indulgent Reader, must be: 'Do what, exactly?' Then he explained how he had come to a decision to put himself forward for selection for the Anglican priesthood.

There are moments in life, apart from drowning, when tremendous amounts of information or memory flash through one's brain. In the space of half a minute I mentally reviewed the leviathan consequences of this notion and then, taking a good lungful of air, I leapt.

'OK then, let's do it,' I said.

If faith and courage are the stuff of what we are dealing in, then faith and courage must be our substance. What I knew would be involved was the loss of privacy, every meal interrupted, the distressed people, the church politics, the pressure on our relationship and no end of God Books. And then there was the stuff that I knew I had no idea about, and nor would I until it cropped up. What I said 'Yes' to that day was the whole shebang.

4

AM I,
BY SOME SLIM CHANCE,
INVOLVED IN THIS?

Well, at least the malaise had a name now. It seems that the usual term for what he was suffering from is a 'Vocation'.

Hitherto I had thought of this as something contagious that Roman Catholic girls in high schools went in dread of catching along with pregnancy. It crops up all the time in Irish novels and stage-plays. I had simply loved watching Diana Rigg in *In this House of Brede* and Jean Simmons in *Black Narcissus* wrestle with it. But it was something no one that I had met outside fiction had ever had. In my agnostic family and my non-denominational private school, one never came into contact with any outbreaks of it. 'Vocation' was a word that conjured up otherness – faint organ music, hushed speaking voices and soft-focus effects. It just didn't happen to the very people that one passes on escalators, or clashes trolleys with in Sainsbury's, or waits with in dentists' surgeries. It just didn't happen in a world of fluorescent lighting, petrol stations, football hooliganism, mutant pigeons and tax returns. It was like finding out that *The Archers* is real.

And here was the person I knew best in the world with an inoperable case of it. Moreover, he himself was only half-pleased by the diagnosis and said that, if he had any choice, he would really rather not have it. I found it a tremendous curiosity.

And, having agreed to seeing it through, I found myself inundated with a prodigious pride in him. I would not understand the half of it, I probably never would. I would muddle through when he was striding ahead but I would never doubt that he was doing what he thought he must. He wanted me along with him, Heaven only knows what for, and I vowed to be there. I would do my very best.

In a way I committed to the marriage that February day in a way I had not on our wedding day. At first I pledged myself to the man – two individuals in a mutually supportive and respectful structure pursuing independent but consciously co-operative paths. Quite neat really and mostly blissfully happy. Now I had pledged myself to something much, much messier – a commonality of purpose in our life together that would involve struggle and forbearance and sacrifice and generosity. The famous Australian cartoonist Michael Leunig has a highly evocative image of life being like a bag of roosters – ungainly and awkward to deal with. The Beloved and I now had a resolve, a vision and our very own bag of roosters.

So there we were, absolutely dripping with hearty zeal and stalwart courage, with no clue as to what would or should happen next. But presently our faith and several phone calls were rewarded and things showed signs of falling into some sort of sequence.

And I found that it was one that mostly left me out of everything. Oh, not in any conscious or pointed way. Just in the way that I was to soon identify as intrinsically C of E – slightly vague, a bit wispy or flabby, studiously inoffensive and something that you can never quite make out clearly enough to put your finger on and have a good air-clearing shouting match about. Tremendously frustrating.

The first thing The Beloved was to do, as we were

advised, was to see the Vicar at All Saints and ask if he thought The Beloved a suitable candidate for sponsorship. That is, was he a goer and how good were the odds?

There began a number of interviews, which The Beloved now began to feel he could be quite open about. The Vicar had a simply vast collection of God Books, and a steady procession of these made their way into the South London flat for visits with the other ones already in residence. Thus we had more God Books than you could poke a stick at, if poking sticks at such things is your idea of fun. We had God Books next to the bed, God Books on the toilet cistern, God Books on the coffee table and God Books in piles next to the front door ready to be returned to make way for some more.

The Beloved was sent off to meet other assessors and advisors, he was pointed in various directions and quizzed searchingly about his progress in this. When he went off to these, I would spend the day wondering with some desperation what was going on, doing slightly compulsive things like scouring round the edges of things with old toothbrushes, frenzied ironing and gnawing my fingernails rather neatly down to the wrist. On his return I would demand that he report every nuance, inflection and hidden subtext of the conversation. I would require action replays that would have been marvellous training for him as a sports commentator were the church to turn him down. And all this was before the poor man had even got his coat off.

The Beloved started formally saying the daily offices of Morning Prayer and Evensong. Just quietly in corners of the sitting room or bedroom, you understand, but the import of this was that there were prayers and stuff going on actually inside the four walls of my home. In my newfound avidity to facilitate the great metamorphosis, I was painfully anxious to give The Beloved the space to do this. I would, upon re-alizing what was happening when the flat went disturbingly quiet, any shouting at radios or mislaid God Books ceased and he disappeared, freeze into clumsy inaction wherever I was so as not to disturb him. I would plunge across the room to turn the radio off, freeze the motion of the sewing machine, wash up with exaggerated delicacy, even turn cooking down so that it didn't sizzle too loudly. I imagined high-powered dialogue and delicate negotiations were going on between God and The Beloved and at no time did I wish to suffer any accusation that I had interrupted or marred anything. There was far too much at stake.

Let me protest, though, that all this change brought very little alteration in The Beloved's demeanour to me. He still met me at the train station, tried to tickle me, held me close at night, argued in the pub, made me tea in bed and swore at politicians. There was no skerrick of evidence of any neglect or oversight – if anything, he was even more loving in his attentions, so overjoyed was he that he had my full support and my conviction that he was doing right.

When our friends began to learn of his intentions, that was when we began to notice that what we were doing scared the willies out of other people, not just us.

The people that first gave some currency to the rumour were friends at church and those on the Greater London Choral Circuit and Grapevine. In my comparatively short time in the country, I had already discovered what a mighty communications network this latter is.

For the edification of the layperson, it comprises all the singers who get paid to sing (or play, in the case of organists) the music for the hundreds of choral services that take place in London every Sunday. They either hold regular positions, which are coveted for the correspondingly regular income and the benefits of first refusal on lucrative weddings or memorial services, or else they function as deputies or 'deps' to the regulars, filling in when they are ill, away or working for someone else for more money. The Circuit workforce is, obviously, fed largely from the chapel choirs and choral scholarships of Oxford or Cambridge or from the music colleges. The work requires nerves of steel as one is constantly 'performing', if such a word is appropriate to acts of worship, music that one has seen for the first time less than an hour previously. There is no time for the nervous, the tentative, the sensitive or the inaccurate. These are the warrior knights of music, their senses and talents honed to a very pointy sharpness. They occasionally refer to each other as 'cowboys', male and female alike, in allusion, perhaps, to some sort of uncharted territory, the ability to shoot from the hip and a pioneering and dare-devil spirit of adventure.

The ways to break into this circuit are not many. One can do the proper thing and audition for the relevant Director of Music. This is only any good to the aspirant if there is a position vacant, if you are enticingly superior to the deps they know already, or if you radiate such youthful prospect and enthusiasm that he (and it usually is a he) will not be able to talk himself out of giving you a chance. Sexual appeal of various sorts may come in handy here, too. The more usual way is to be lassooed in by your mates already in there.

Once I had gained my much-coveted regular position, through the rare but sober channel of being on the spot when a position fell vacant, I began to realize the immensity of The Circuit. The best thing to do to learn about it, and to be involved in any enterprises or considered for any work going, was to drink with it. More accurately to get regularly very drunk with its members and thus become partner to whatever scrapes and japes occur as a result. It is folly, unless your career is so overwhelmingly busy that you don't give a monkey's, to meet any member of The Circuit without carrying your diary and a list of the phone numbers of your own mates who it would be feasible to rope into anything going.

A typical post-service pub session will comprise about 10 to 15 minutes (approximately one round) of general revision of the occasion to the effect of 'Did anyone time that maundering sermon?'; 'What about Benny's burp in bar 48?'; and 'Has anyone got 16 across yet?' There will follow a citation of cricket or football scores highlighting particular unlikely goals or superhuman shots. Talk will next turn to who has been asked to do Old Teflon's Bach B Minor next Thursday and then somebody will ask if you have your diary with you. It is vital not to fail yourself at this point with vague I've-Left-It-At-Home-Today's. When you have answered the enquiry as to your availability or, indeed, inclination and ascertained the paucity of the fee, it is then proper to either offer to buy the next round or to plead Sunday lunch and depart. However, should you choose the latter gambit, you will be fatally in the dark about what happens later in the session and thus not have a clue as to why everyone is stifling hysterical giggles all through Evensong.

It is no exaggeration to say that the contacts I made in my first involvement with The Circuit still keep me in work to this day and the friends made then are those which I would still call my closest. I have no doubt that we will all grow decrepit together, staggering still from church to pub to curryhouse and recounting the glory days of improvising alternative verses to *The Church's One Salvation* and recalling the effects of 12 drunken basses on historic masonry.

So it was these friends that got wind of The Beloved's intentions first. Being quite comfortable in church and around church people they were, for the most part, delighted and excited. Those that were more dubious about his prospects took the chance to have finger-waving discussions in various public houses with him. Consequently the news flashed across the network with the lightning rapidity that marks the process of any juicy morsel.

All the while The Beloved was being discussed with, challenged, probed, opened up, channelled, explored, assessed and so thoroughly supported on this life-changing journey by all the C of E Powers-That-Be, the only thing I was generally asked is, 'Isn't it all exciting?'

Yes, it is exciting. It is as exciting as it is bewildering, maddening, worrying and confusing. And only a very few people ever asked me, 'What do *you* think about all this?', 'Is it upsetting you?', 'Can I do anything for you?', 'Are you all right?', 'Why don't I take you to the pub, you can have a good panic and then we'll get legless and giggle and shriek a lot.' The ones that did, particularly the ones that performed the latter invaluable function, are terrestrial saints. Probably martyrs too by the time they lovingly sat through my lengthy accounts of telephone gaffes with bishops' advisors and sweaty nightmares about parish toddler groups and kitchen disposal units.

The friends that were not so much involved with church or choral music were the ones that found out next. These then, quite quickly, divided themselves into three sub-groups. The first sort were the ones that stopped swearing when in my company or started apologizing for doing so. Among the dubious benefits of a career in performing is an easy command of the bluer forms of expression. In Oz creative swearing and insult is virtually an artform in its own right, its practitioners much admired and emulated. I should mention here that The Beloved holds the equivalent of a PhD in this discipline, another of his eclectic talents. So when those colleagues, who would not normally dream of censoring their turns of phrase in everyday interaction, began to do so whenever I was around, I felt that I had been removed from some sort of area of acceptability. I was someone with whom one had to watch Ps and Qs, someone for whom dusting and tidying occurred before a visit, someone with whom they were no longer relaxed and easy.

And I felt hurt and sorry, usually, that a camaraderie was ended, that a certain properness and censoriousness was suddenly assumed of me. And that this way of interacting with me was more acceptable than with the reality of my actual personality. I occasionally found myself being even more extravagant in my manner in the hope, I suppose, of breaking through the assumption and regaining that lost acceptance. And then I felt even sadder that I had had to.

The second sort remained mostly unchanged in my solo company but when The Beloved was with me they would exhibit certain signs of social discomfort. Consciously or unconsciously the topic of conversation would be steered around to their own dreadful religious schooling or awful experiences with sadistic clergymen. All we heard about for months were their reasons for not going to church themselves or their repeated apologies for espousing views which they perceived to be other than Christian ones. It was as if they had forgotten that we could discuss ideas, art, causes, jokes, theatre, gossip, parties.

The third sort were the saddest sort of all. They just decided, usually without any notification, that we had turned into complete nerds and they faded themselves out of our lives, except for occasional apologetic I'm-So-Terribly-Busy Christmas cards. I can only suppose these thought we had gone over to some sort of opposition, that we had joined an enemy, that we had betrayed something.

The most difficult factor about all three groups was that their decisions or assumptions were made on the basis of their own fears or hang-ups, without any consultation, warning or any seeming fidelity to the people they knew either of us to be 'before'.

That single word, Vocation, meant that I now had a myriad of mal-informed suppositions made about me and most of these were wrong.

5

BEING IGNORED (1)

I was now beginning to understand what it was likely to be like for the rest of my life. It seems I was to live with any number of inaccurate suppositions about me, from both those within the dear old C of E and any general public. My opinion was never going to be sought and I was rarely to be consulted in any matter. I had always heard about poor, shadowy clergy wives, down-trodden in this way and I always wondered why on earth they put up with it. Many of my generation were reared by mothers who burnt their bras, staged sit-ins, pioneered contraception and did the go-go. Surely, surely nowadays we knew better than that. But the wisdom that experience was beginning to teach me was that there was absolutely nothing I could do about it. Really, absolutely nothing. It did not stop or go away. I could have been a Company Director, a pop star or an MP and still I was inexorably headed for the anonymous status of a message-taking, tea-making adjunct to the vicar. A mere vegetable side-dish to The Beloved's beef vindaloo.

The egocentricity of the performer did not sit well with this. The egocentricity of the performer is sensitive to being overlooked. The egocentricity of this performer swung wildly between figurative kicking and screaming and snooty aloofness to it all. Either I would comment with the slicing tongue that is mine when angered or just pity people for not knowing any better.

This basic paradigm shift in how people perceived me, or didn't as the case more often was, is something about which I would warn anyone whose partner has caught some sort of Vocation. My hope is that being forewarned may lessen the shock of onset, even if it cannot make it any more palatable. Let it get to you and it can put some pretty massive dents in your self-confidence, your home life and your attitude to your partner's ministry.

The Beloved, while being generous, understanding and moderate with me, was also no slouch in fighting my cause when he could. He would patiently and with that hint of steel, point out to people filling in forms or writing name tags that we have different names and that I am not Mrs anybody. On one occasion, when a receptionist was prevented from adhering a sticky label with the wrong name to my unwitting jacket lapel for this reason, she replied, 'Oh, but how will we know who you are?' How, indeed?

When asked in interviews that curly one about whether his wife 'supported' his decision to go forward for selection, he would politely say that this was for his wife to answer herself and remind them of our telephone number.

And all the while that this 'support' of mine was referred to in my absence, I was wondering what 'support' was actually supposed to entail. Was I meant to act as a counsellor, discussing the aspects of the process in a warm and soft voice while nodding a lot? Was I meant to be a sounding-board, play devil's advocate and, in rabbinical tradition, counter him in everything? Was I meant to just silently exude great wafts of approbation? Was I to become some sort of girdle or corset or splint or zimmer frame? Or was I just to shut up and pay the bills?

Not having any ready-made clue as to the correct answer, I did all of these at the times I thought appropriate and, as The Beloved seemed to be happy, that is the way it was.

The families in Oz had to be told of what was happening. In the case of mine, the fateful letters elicited bemused surprise from most of them and a surprisingly knowing and warm commendation from my mother. The Beloved's family was a bit more of a minefield. His committed, practising Roman Catholic mother and his papally knighted father took it very hard. His brothers and sisters mostly felt confirmed in their belief that he is potty – loveable but potty. The isolation from them made it both easy and hard. Easy in that there were no rows or haranguing matches, no bitterness over the breakfast table. Hard in that there was little explanation possible. After two or three feeling letters from his father eloquently arguing the seriousness of The Beloved's betrayal of the One True Faith, the subject was mostly avoided completely.

And all the time the dear old C of E continued to grind its way to a decision about The Beloved. And all the same time I painfully learnt how to wait. How to wait for appointments, how to wait for letters, how to wait for forms to leave one office and to arrive at another, how to wait for reports to be consulted, how to wait for telephone calls to be returned, and so on, and so on. While I am generally thought of as abounding in energetic and purposeful qualities, I am not normally considered to be unusually impatient. But here I was called to perfect a skill I had more than an inkling I would call upon a lot in times to come. This was, and is, largely due to an under-researched but commonly prevalent phenomenon in time, perception and relativity. Time in the Church of England does not run like time in the rest of creation. And no amount of trying, however ingenious or forceful, to bring the two into parallel will prevail.

There are a number of elements to the skill of Waiting. Patience does not drop tinkling and sparkly from the skies like Cinderella's ballgown. It has to be studied and mastered.

The first lesson is in dealing with frustration. Apart from the obvious and tremendously gratifying recourse of kicking something, the thing to do is dissect what it is that is actually frustrating you. Rather than let a huge and amorphous frustration sit on your digestion like a stone, defuse this by breaking it down into component parts.

You are either being inadvertently or deliberately frustrated. If it is deliberate then be clear that it is someone else who is culpable and you should not indulge in knocking yourself for not coping well. It is either that the frustrator is malicious, in which case you should not dream of gratifying them by rising to it; or else it is some sort of twisted test, in which case you should prove beyond doubt your laudable self-mastery and completely ignore it. If, on the other hand, it is inadvertent, the problem does enter into your domain. The easiest, but not entirely charitable, method of dealing with it is to assume that your frustrator is a half-wit and has no inkling of what they are doing. The other involves rather energetic exercises in humility and means admitting to yourself that you actually are unreasonably impatient, you have got it very badly wrong, you have missed the vital point, you simply don't understand or that you are the half-wit.

The next lesson is in dealing with the anger that the frustration engenders. Breaking things and shouting naughty words is quite effective, as is weeping, biting your nails, chewing your hair and sulking. May I suggest, though, that perhaps a more positive use of this energy is to chop up a lot of vegetables with a large kitchen knife or cleaver, hang all the rugs on the clothes line and beat the hell out of them, write a filthy letter to the company that runs your local bus service, or dig all those waist-high brambles from the bottom of the garden. Go for a five-mile hike, take your credit card for a jaunt to the West End, or just open that Bolly that you've been saving since you forgot your anniversary. Whatever your preferred means, it is important to diffuse the anger so that it is not bottled up or thrown unfairly in the face of an innocent bystanding party.

Lesson number three in Waiting is in delegation. In the world there are two categories of things – things to worry about and things not to worry about. You will do yourself a great favour if you can decide, in as business-like fashion as you can, which are which and then either worry with full, brow-knitted commitment or don't. Messy, untidy or dilatory worrying is a terrible waste of energy.

And the final lesson in the course is in acceptance – acceptance that the frustration has occurred or is occurring, that you have done all you can about it and there is nothing more that your efforts can achieve. This, too, has various facets. There is dignified acceptance, grudging acceptance, distracted acceptance, resigned acceptance and smiling acceptance. All of these are suitable at various times, depending on the individual circumstances, your mood, your blood sugar level, whether the loo seat was left up or down and the phases of the moon. If you have worked your way through to this final lesson, you may consider yourself to have mastered waiting. You may, like me, never actually be very brilliant at it, but at least you will know more about it and how to go about doing it with confidence.

I was to have a good 18 months of intensive study and practice before The Beloved actually got to his selection conference. But I must not leap ahead of myself and you, indulgent Reader, will have to wait for future chapters to know about that. You could cheat, I suppose, and thumb forward a couple of chapters but you would miss such diverting portions of sub-plot and background that it would simply be no fun.

That summer brought a number of lovely things to offset the Waiting. First, one of the most notorious of choral cowboys known to us all decided to get a bunch of us together for a jolly. This served the dual purposes of exercising his own abundant conducting abilities and concurrently providing all the music for the daily sung services in Hereford cathedral for the period of a week, the resident choir being on summer holiday. A massive choir of nearly 40 professionals from the GLCCG willingly volunteered. One could almost say that there was a stampede to postboxes all over London in order to get replies to the invitations returned. The Beloved was allowed to join us as an honorary cowboy and organist's page-turner. For some reason, yet unfathomed, the unsuspecting cathedral chapter decided to allow us in and we were allotted the whole of the boys' old school for our accommodation. Into these hallowed halls we brought our sleeping bags, our sharpened pencils, two crates of gin, three of tonic and a bag of lemons. We were going to call ourselves *Cantores Armentarii* but, realizing that the Precentor's Latin might be up to recognizing that meant *The Singing Cowboys*, the more sedate *Clemens Non Papa Singers* was arrived at.

Rehearsals were to be daily at ten o'clock until lunch and then at four o'clock until we sang Evensong at five. In between and thereafter our time was our own to fill as we chose. We chose the usual pastimes peculiar to a period of glorious English summer weather – eating, drinking, sitting on lawns or the outdoor furniture provided by local hostelries and wearing skimpy sundresses and comical shorts. As a result we got drunk, sunburnt, thrown out of two restaurants, barred from three pubs and carpeted by the Precentor for singing Tallis at the tops of our voices in the Close at four o'clock one morning. But in the choirstalls, we produced some of the finest and most enthusiastic renditions of choral classics that have echoed round those ancient pillars for a long while. And it wasn't just us that said so. In a speech of departure the Precentor was generous enough to say that, though we were the most unruly visiting choir he had ever had to deal with, we were undeniably the best.

Not long after we returned to London, and amid yet more choral extravagance, The Beloved and I had our marriage blessed in church at All Saints. To do this was an idea that had formed only gradually as we brought it up in conversation from time to time and then left it alone again. It grew from the feeling that, now there was this new dimension or impetus to our relationship, now that we were 'us' in a different way, we wanted it recognized and formalized in a renewed covenant. While none of our families could be there for the obvious reasons of proximity, or a lack thereof, we had a good, hearty churchful of mates who celebrated with us with a will.

There was further good news when I learned that I had weathered a handful of auditions and secured my first real opera contract. I was to start rehearsals in December and tour for six months in my first operatic rôle since student productions at university, almost ten years previously.

This could not have happened at a better time for us financially. We were just getting to the stage where we were scraping the barrel of our savings and I was ringing the Art schools and offering myself as a Life Class model. I thought, if all else fails I could always take my clothes off. I thought I would actually be quite good at this, having spent a lot of time when younger modelling for my mother and never having suffered from an overly meagre figure. Through my dancing days this had been a source of some anguish but now I thought my experience and my pneumatic charms would qualify me sufficiently to earn the hourly sitting rate. However, this opera contract was secured and I would be singing Mozart for our supper instead. Probably just as well, really. I mean, think of what would happen if The Beloved eventually became a bishop and then some ghastly tabloid reproduced ancient sketches of me in a native state. It would either ruin him – or add hugely to his credibility.

But no. It seems we were destined to follow a comparatively virtuous life. We couldn't help but feel that we were doing something right somewhere.

6

BEING INSPECTED

Up to this point, Waiting aside, I had had it easy. Apart from a bit of a cordial chat and a highly civilized lunch with our vicar, I had not really become a figure in the vocational equation. Any consideration of me, as attached to The Beloved, had been at a somewhat genteel distance. Either I was glaringly obviously the perfect prospective clergy wife and no more needed to be said about it or, more realistically, the item on the Church of England's 'must do' list that says 'Suss out what the wife thinks and see if she'll be any good' was not very far from the bottom. In fact I'm pretty sure it was a long way below 'Try to make sense of Synod', 'Ban all nylon-stringed guitars from places of worship', 'Find a groovy press image for the Archbishop' and 'Deal with international debt, famine and human rights violations'.

However, now the spotlight was to turn on me. Or was it a searchlight? An ominous and immovable appointment was shakily scrawled into my diary. The dread day of meeting the Diocesan Director of Ordinands loomed blacker than the dentist.

As I have already discussed, I had become increasingly impatient with the grinding slowness with which the Church of England's machinery seems to work. Any movement in the direction we were so eager to go took for ever. We were poised on the starting blocks but the starter had either left his pistol in the drawer at home in Cornwall or needed 14 committee meetings to get permission to fire it – and then only if there was an R in the month.

Our work situation, due to the undecided nature of the future, was not what anyone would blithely describe as 'stable' or 'normal'. Here was I working 12-hour days and selling my car to pay the rent, while The guilt-racked Beloved was unable to consider taking a proper job because at any moment that earth-shattering call may come and he would zoom away to a selection conference. And, should he clear that hurdle, he could be – I'm sorry, *we* could be – at college within a short, fraught six months.

I say again, time in the Church of England does not run like time in the rest of creation.

So I was soldiering on. I won't say that I was doing this quietly and self-effacingly. All studies in Waiting apart, I wasn't doing this in a subtle manner. My good friends know that suffering in the background is not one of my numerous talents, nor is doing anything quietly. I can, if asked, make washing-up or tea-making into a quite diverting four act opera.

My valiant soldiering at that time involved waiting tables for a peanut per hour in the local restaurant run by an appallingly sexist manager, as well as stitching what seemed like hundreds of costumes for a theatre school's end-of-year blockbuster showcase. As I stuffed yards of tulle and cerise-coloured lining satin through the sewing machine by day and evaded the groping hands on both sides of the bar by night, I wrote and rehearsed the terse little speech I was going to deliver to the DDO.

I was going to make it crystal clear to this Very Important Man just how close we were to severe financial difficulties if the dear old C of E didn't get a bit of a wriggle on. I was going to protest warmly at the somewhat blasé way the dear old C of E assumed that partners, and in particular this wife, would carry the can without even asking if that partner, or this particular wife, minded. I was going to point out in absolutely certain terms that there was only so long a body could work the hours that I did and retain the sunny charm and unfailingly cheerful outlook that had hitherto been known as an integral part of my personality. I was going to say that, if something didn't happen rather soon, I was going to rip his head off.

I marched down the street to the DDO's house on the fateful evening with a thin veneer of civility masking a pathological need to maim. I was ready to commence this battle with all my well-rehearsed armaments blazing. I neither noticed the pleasant treelined way or The Beloved trying to talk conciliatory sense to me. After a tense half-minute on the doorstep during which I reassuringly hissed that I was '*Fine*, really, just *FINE*, okay?', the door swung open.

It swung open with such force that I was almost sucked into the hallway. But a counterblast came in a loud and cheerful voice. 'Great news!' it boomed. 'All systems are go! Your conference is on 18 March! You must be Adey! *Do* come in!'

I deflated like a released balloon and felt thoroughly foolish and ready to cry. I was also, now that I was no longer on the offensive, really frightened.

It is a nasty, but regular, part of my job as a performer to go to interviews or auditions. I try to convince people that I am exactly the sort of person that is wanted for the rôle. I am a 'find'. I am the quintessential comic relief, winsome lover, battered wife, cheeky principal boy, or feisty working girl.

The big difference between that and now was that I was not up for a role. I had no character research or plot background to fall back on. And what the hell are the identifiable qualities of a Potential Ordinand's Significant Other anyway? What was of interest here, even grave importance, was not what I could do but who I was. The trouble was that 'me' was, and still is, a really useful resource when building a character or interpreting text or music but if looked at too closely was, and still is, revealed to be the usual, mortal, rather unsightly mess of insecurities. And I was about to be closely looked at.

Trying to tell myself to get something more like an iron grip on my wobbly diaphragm and my suddenly minimal lung capacity, we picked through the bomb-site of what was left of a meal with small children. We sashayed through the toys, mushy peas and marker pens into an office where we were invited to sit down. I took a deep breath.

This was the first time I had encountered what has come to be very familiar. What I now faced was a handy-wipe-clean-leatherette Church of England Armchair. Let me describe the effects of contact with these contraptions:

After placing oneself in the habitual position preparatory to sitting there is a dangerously rapid reverse descent, a bounce and an unsettling equal and opposite dynamic reaction resulting from the seat of the Armchair being a good eight inches lower than it looks to the untrained or inexperienced eye. Your knees are now above your heart. Sitting with any grace or poise (and for women this usually means keeping your knees together) is only possible in two positions. The first, known as the Perch, is sitting on the very front edge of the Armchair. A brisk but surreptitious wriggle is required to attain this position after initially floundering about with your bottom further back on the seat. The more experienced Armchair-sitter will be able to use the bounce and the equal and opposite dynamic reaction to propel themselves quickly to the front of the Armchair after the initial descent.

The second, the Lounge, is achieved after the initial bounce has subsided and requires leaning back until one's shoulders make contact with the back of the Armchair, thus rendering one's trunk virtually supine as this, again, is a much greater distance than the eye would perceive. It is now permissible to adjust any scatter-cushions provided or even put them on the floor if you do not need them to prop yourself into a position where the air may pass freely up and down your windpipe. Cross your legs and use one elbow on an armrest to prevent complete subsidence.

There is a third position, known as the Basic, where the bottom is placed in the centre of the seat, the bent knees are spread with the feet flat on the floor and the forearms or hands rest on the knees. But this latter is usually only used by men because they are wearing trousers or women who don't mind about keeping their knees together.

Escape from an Armchair requires a threefold action. A heaving convulsion, a mighty muscular clench and a suppressed grunt may usually be combined to make it possible to stand upright again. The less fit may find they have to repeat any of these three a few times to achieve verticality. Try to make the actions flow as smoothly as possible and remember that giggling or squealing uses up precious breath. Think of the Olympic parallel bars, focus and concentrate.

I now nurture a theory that there is a manufacturing company, probably somewhere in Norfolk, that makes Armchairs to precise C of E specifications down to the one dodgy spring and the farty noises built into the seat.

Ensconced in a magnificent example of an Armchair – I was affecting the Perch to begin with – I took in the room over the rim of my kitchen tumbler of (very good) red wine. The wallpapered walls were mercifully camouflaged with books, the curtains were terylene of a colour so frightening they deserved an X-rating and the carpet was a brown and orange nylon 'curry' design. The desk was hidden under dozens of foot-high piles of papers. This guy, apart from being a VIM, was obviously a Very Busy Man.

It started out well. Easy conversation between the VIM

and The Beloved flowed. I think The Beloved was even moving towards the Lounge (having begun in the Basic) when the spotlight turned directly onto me. I brought into employment all the lessons a life in the theatre had taught me about how to seem confident, calm and assured. Keep your voice low, don't laugh too much, watch your body language, remember his name, make eye-contact often, watch that your skirt doesn't ride up, don't drink the wine too fast, don't wave your hands around too much, don't spill the wine, don't say 'um', don't fiddle with your hair, put the bloody wine down, sit up straight and concentrate, etc., etc. In actors' speak this is called the 'third eye' and is a valuable function to acquire and to be able to call up. It means that both hemispheres of the brain are functioning at once. You are emoting your socks off while monitoring technical control of the instrument. I was in marvellous technical control of my instrument. I recall the exertion of remembering all these auto-instructions and putting them into effective action. Unfortunately, I have very little memory of what the VBM actually asked me.

My single clear recollection is of when he asked me about my 'support' of The Beloved's Vocation. I launched into a moving homily about my trust in his conviction. I declared a fierce pride in his courage. I declaimed a readiness to move Heaven and earth to allow him to realize his aims. I admitted a willingness to iron his clerical shirts and answer the door 70 times seven a day. I think I even mentioned God somewhere.

'How touching,' DDO/VIM/VBM said. He was looking at me with a mixture of confusion, amusement and admiration.

I then realized that all I was really being asked about was my income.

I was later informed by The Beloved that I was asked a number of other pretty telling questions which I had the absent presence of mind to answer with great honesty. These apparently covered topics such as our plans concerning children, whether we were here in the UK to stay and how we dealt with our families on the other side of the world. Among these was also the biggie about how we would deal with moving house every few years. Now for one opera singer and one actor/writer this, I can assure you, is chickenfeed. Since we had met, The Beloved and I had lived at nine addresses and have since added five to that number. My friends will attest to the assistance of a small instruction booklet I have written on the subject. Baby, we move house like other people have hot dinners.

So I was grilled, stir-fried and probably lightly boiled as well by Acronym Man. After an unknowable aeon, we said our goodbyes and The Beloved and I marched wordlessly, shoulder-to-shoulder, in an all but perfectly straight line, to the nearest pub. We only made eye-contact once we were safely positioned behind two great big pints. We solemnly ingested two packets of crisps each and then My Beloved spake and said unto me, 'Well, you only said "f★★k" five times.'

7

THE LONELINESS OF THE LONG-DISTANCE SPOUSE

I was subsequently provided with further, and even more comprehensive, opportunities to practise my studied skills in Waiting. Indeed, I can say that I was able to hone these skills to points of such fineness that they would probably only be visible under a microscope. The dear old C of E is inordinately generous in this regard.

I had by now commenced the long and, consequently, mercifully lucrative opera contract. This company toured two productions at once with the principals of one singing the chorus parts for the other. I was playing First Boy in *The Magic Flute* and swanning around in the crowd scenes of *Don Pasquale*.

When I was about eight years old my ballet school put on a production of *Coppelia*. My father played Dr Coppelius and I was a small boy in the toyshop. I was appealingly costumed in a little sailor suit and straw hat and looked cheeky and adorable. I was photographed in our back garden in this garb, grinning in a way that I am told won many hearts. Twenty years later I found myself, as First Boy, appealingly costumed in a little sailor suit and looking as cheeky and adorable as one can when one is a good 20 years older than the character is. I had my friend Margaret, the Third Boy, photograph me in a similar pose to the childhood original for the amusement of my parents. I laughed to see that, despite the rigours of adolescence, a degree in music and the sheer weight of 20 years (most of which seems to have settled round the hips and inner thighs), the grin remains the same.

The *Don Pasquale* production, however, was to be set in Rome in the 1950s and I was one of a couple of girls chosen to lounge about the 'pool' while Norina walloped her way through her big aria and generally introduced herself to audiences three times a week. So it was that, of all the strange ways I have found myself earning a living, I was dressed in nothing but a beautiful, original 50s swimming costume, false eyelashes and a couple of hair slides, lying still for eight minutes at a time during an early spring that saw the UK engulfed in some of the worst icy weather and snowstorms it had seen for 20 years. I can assure my gentle Reader I was not aglow with anything but chilblains.

The snow had got so bad on the day of the opening night in Swindon that the Tamino, Papageno, Pamina and myself, who had taken an idyllic country cottage together, were obliged to dig the car out of the idyllic country snowdrifts in our idyllic country lane every six metres to get to the main road and thus to the theatre for the show. Our landlady had helpfully provided us with wellies and shovels which we stashed in the boot of the car along with a couple of duvets and a bottle and a half of whiskey. Our thoughts were that, should the cream of young operatic talent die of exposure in a snowstorm, they would want to go as drunk as possible.

However, originating from a place where one rarely sees any snow, never mind has to deal with it in any quantities, I was having a complete ball in it all. Also I was deriving no small amount of amusement from the panic that seemed to engulf not only my colleagues but the entire country. It struck me (and still does) as delightful that a meteorological phenomenon that has, at a good guess, been occurring in this country since the first Ice Age could so alarm the whole populace, preoccupying their every mental function. But then, of course, I am foreign and just don't understand these things.

The bonus for exposing myself to the dangers of hypothermia three times a week was a jolly good one though. In the last act of *Don Pasquale* I was supposed to be a party guest and for the occasion was poured into a simply stunning strapless evening dress made of leopard-skin print lamé and worn with shoulder-length black evening gloves. The chorus has only about 16 bars to sing in this scene, at the very end as a final blast before the curtain, and we spent the rest of the time looking variously busy, purposeful, enraptured, overwhelmed with hilarity and generally decorating the set. I am quite sure that the only reason that I was put in the scene at all was to parade this creation across the stage half a dozen times for the deserved greater glory of the designer. It certainly beat waiting tables.

All this meant that I was away from home for six days a week. The Beloved continued to work all the freelance radio shifts he could and set himself up writing at home in between. This latter occupation set him a small practical challenge that he rose to with his usual individual ingenuity.

In all this snow and icy weather, we could by no means afford to have the heating on all day. In our financially pared-down state we were still terrified of running up the bills, even after I had got such a good contract. So The Beloved spent his days giving birth to his latest fiery wordplay dressed in the following wise: additional to his usual underwear were long-sleeved T-shirt and long johns (in a delicate shade of pink since their washing disaster with a red T-shirt), thick lumberjack shirt, red flannel bush-shirt, jeans, red woollen jumper, thicker green woollen jumper, bright blue leg-warmers, khaki balaclava, red fingerless mittens and pink floral duvet over the knees. I came home one afternoon (having not perished in a snowstorm) to find him hard at work in this costume, bashing and swearing at the typewriter in the fashion that creates all good literature, and methought once more what a good-hearted and interesting person he was to live with.

It was dressed sensibly otherwise, though, that he went off to his selection conference. The then Bishop of London had told him that The Beloved had the questionable honour of being his last sponsored candidate before his retirement. Aware of some import in this, The Beloved had been worded-up by the Vicar and Simon and pep-talked by DDO/VIM/VBM and, all in all, seemed fully primed to be fired out of the churchly cannon into pastures unknown and scary. We had pored over the timetable for the conference's three days, trying to formulate possible questions and situations and The Beloved's consequent answers and responses. It seemed, from reference to friends and supporters, that it was all right to go for a drink in the evening in a social sort of manner but not to let off steam there in any uncontrolled way. It was all right to express firm opinions as long as they didn't threaten or upset anyone else's firmly held opinions. One was to be honest and open about all aspects of one's person without tending towards self-advertisement. One was to dress normally and sensibly without displaying too many of one's fashion-victim tendencies. And one was to avoid, at all costs, one terrifying mistake.

According to the suggestions as to demeanour on the papers, there were many blunders that candidates may find themselves committing for reasons of nervousness or social ineptitude but these would, on the whole, most probably provide useful and telling insights for the selectors, so we were not to get too uptight. However, the single crime that it was advised to shun completely, the worst of them all, was Vapid Hilarity.

Having obtained a translation as to what this serious *faux-pas* actually entailed, The Beloved felt himself as prepared as anyone could be for a three-day third-degree.

It is a fact that The Beloved is perfectly capable of putting a few essential things in an overnight bag. I, however, am usually unable to believe this and so take the task on myself, knowing that only then will I sleep lonely, but secure, in the knowledge that his socks have no holes in them, his shirts are ironed and he has his toothbrush and some clean pants. In this case there was very little else I could do for him apart from this and so I got full mileage out of worrying whether he needed to take a towel and whether he should wear a tie to dinner.

Thankfully I was away working before and on the actual days of his conference but they were preceded by several of those agonizing phone calls of very little content apart from me telling him that I loved him very much and that he mustn't shout at any biblical fundamentalists.

So off he went and three days of a knotted stomach and consequent trapped wind ensued. For me that was, not him. He returned under the impression that he had been reasonably relaxed, honest and comprehensive in his responses. Generally he felt he had given a good strong, clear account of himself. By the grace of God he had avoided Vapid Hilarity.

Subsequently though, the inevitable happened and insidious self-dissection began. In the ensuing agonizing weeks of waiting for a verdict, we pressed the action replay button over every moment of the 72 hours he had been in the searchlight's glare. This can get pretty severe when the activity is stretched over a long period of time. We became increasingly convinced that he had said the wrong thing in every situation, trodden on every toe and, all in all, that he had blown it.

To add to the angst, the Bishop insisted on marking the

verdict on his last sponsored candidate by telling him of it in person. The letter from the conference selection panel would be forwarded to him and The Beloved was to make an appointment to hear its contents with his very own ears. And, the Bishop being another VBM, these appointments didn't grow on trees. This was the reason that it was not until four weeks after the conference that The Beloved could know the actuality of his ignominious failure.

During the third of these weeks a slightly strange meeting occurred. The operas were playing Lincoln and The Beloved had decided to give himself a little holiday and come with me. We had lovely digs at the top of Steep Hill (and it is wise to believe those who tell you just how steep it is) not far from the cathedral. We had spent a wonderful wind-blown day climbing all over the ruins of the old Bishop's Palace and, having taken tea in the cathedral's fine tearooms, attended Evensong. I then went on to the theatre where The Beloved, who had a seat to see the show, would meet me later.

Mingling with the appreciative interval crowds and wrestling towards the bar intent upon gin, he came face to face with the senior of his conference selection panel. She beamed at him and cheerfully said, 'Hello there! What are you doing here?'

The Beloved explained that his wife was the First of the sailor-suited Boys.

'How lovely! Now, have you heard yet?'

The Beloved, not a little tense about the matter, replied in the negative.

'Ah! Then I don't think I can talk to you.'

She then smiled warmly again and drifted away on the tide of the crowd. All this The Beloved related to me later and finally, neither of us knowing what to make of the encounter, we settled down to the last few days of agony with a certain jaw-set grimness.

I was playing the northern market town of Darlington the week that the will of the Lord was due to be made known via the selectors, Royal Mail and the Bishop of London. It was April and in the still chilly winds the daffodils were all up and waving and trees were blooming but I didn't know whether to let this cheer me or not. On the day that our torment was to be over, The Beloved had his appointment to see the Bishop in the morning. We had arranged that I would telephone later that afternoon, on my way to the theatre, and learn the news.

The phone box that I had found to be the best isolated from traffic noise was in the churchyard of St Cuthbert's, the ancient parish church of the town. It sits in a dell of flowerbeds and leaning tombstones all neatly kept. It is a strong, old, medieval building with buttresses and a finely pointed spire. I passed it on my way to the theatre and thus had found the phone box. And in this phone box I stood that afternoon shaking with cold and fright. The voice of The Beloved, sounding tight-throated and suspiciously casual at the same time, said, 'The answer's Yes.'

I didn't understand. So prepared was I for major disappointment and for supporting The Beloved through it that an affirmative answer didn't appear in the script that I had rehearsed. 'Yes! Yes to what?'

'I'm through. I start college in September.'

One of those strange moments happened when the whole world suddenly stops. The wind momentarily dropped and there was a lull in the traffic. Then, all of a sudden, the spring sun broke through the clouds and my swimming eyes were filled with the blinding gold of the daffodils. At the same minute, in the church tower, the bell-ringers commenced their weekly practice and the wild crash of their peals shook the ground and made me all but deaf with their glory.

Shakily I managed to convey to The Beloved how ecstatic

and proud I was and told him that, in case he hadn't noticed it yet, I loved him very much.

I hung up and sat on the floor of the phone box. Eighteen months of uncertainty, suspense, irresolution and dogged perseverance were suddenly over. Looking through the glass at the bright trumpeting of the daffs, my ears full of the ringing of the bells, I cried and cried and cried.

Having picked myself up, blown my nose, realized that I was late and assured a kind passing lady that I was fine, really, I had just received some very good news that was all, I started running towards the theatre.

At the edge of the churchyard two thoughts pulled me up short. The first was to send a hasty, but no less heartfelt, thankyou upwards. The second was that I would now probably spend the rest of my days living within the glorious sound of bells.

8

NO ROOM TO
SWING THE CAT

So, after so long, we suddenly were blessed with a lavish richness of plans, deadlines, decisions and an awful lot to organize.

The first and most telling thing to decide was where
The Beloved was going to go to college. This had to be
flavoured variously by thoughts of what he thought he
wanted to do academically, what the spiritual life of the place
was like and how they did it, were the other ordinands the
sort of people with whom he could be pleasantly cheek-by-
jowl, and where could he stash the wife for a couple of years.

Being older than the average ordinand, The Beloved was
deemed much more sensible and down-to-earth and simply
dripping with 'life experience'. It was thus decided by the
Powers-That-Be that he should jog briskly through college
training and complete a two-year certificate rather than waste
any precious time lolling around, indulgently enjoying himself in the pastures of theological academe. The colleges that
offered this course where a good Anglo-Catholic lad might
feel right at home were not numerous and The Beloved
eventually settled on a list of three to view – a certain one in
Cambridge, a certain one in Oxford and another certain one
not a very long way from Oxford. Appointments to visit each
place were made and entered into diaries in big letters.

The next thing to decide was what we should do with
the large terrace house we still owned in Sydney and all our

goods and chattels that had been in storage for three years. It seemed, by now, that we were plumping for residence in the UK in a somewhat permanent fashion and it struck us that there was little point to everything we owned being 12,000 miles away. Accordingly we made the phone call to the storage company to stick it all on a ship coming in this direction and The Beloved put himself on an aeroplane going in the other. As I was still touring the sailor suit and the swimming costume around and we couldn't afford two fares, he went on his own with the simple snip of a brief to wind up the tenants' agreement, paint the house, sell the house, close all our bank accounts, close our tax files, organize a power of attorney and pull the plug on our pension plans. Serious global migrational stuff. Easy.

All this The remarkable Beloved accomplished in a month and was back in Blighty to do his college visits in June. Let me say once more what an amazing chap he is.

During our visit to the college in Oxford, after we had been shown around by friends who were already resident there, been talked through the timetable and found out something about financial arrangements, we wound up in the Principal's office. Of course, I was a little more practised at the handy-wipe-clean-leatherette Church of England Armchair nowadays and faultlessly manoeuvred into The Perch. From here I could most easily manage the firebucket of dry sherry that I had been handed on entry, putting it on the floor or bringing it to my lips without too much effort or any grunting.

After The Beloved had been fully interrogated, the Principal turned to me and said, 'So you're a singer! Well, it *will* be lovely to have a good voice in church on Sundays.'

I stopped with the firebucket in mid-air. Once more I sighed at the unthinking assumption that I would believe what my Beloved believes, practise those beliefs as my

Beloved does and have no thoughts, passions, diary dates or culinary preferences that are not the same as his. I covered a look of some exasperation by placing the firebucket carefully on the floor. 'I'm sorry, Father, but people usually pay me to go to church if they want me to sing. It's my job, you see.'

I don't know why this is such a hard concept to grasp or why it comes as such a surprise that singers actually need paying in money for their work. Let's face it, they train for years, live with all sorts of rigours and deprivations to maintain the instrument in peak condition and then get paid peanuts anyway if their name is not Kiri or Luciano. And yet it is not an uncommon assumption that giving vent to a tune or two is something that we simply can't stop ourselves doing and we spend our lives in a state of cheerful warbling. I can assure my gentle Reader that, while it is a great joy and inspiration to have as a profession something as interesting as music, there are occasional times when I would rather stick pins in my eyes than sing.

The Principal went a bit pink and harrumphed and The Beloved saved the moment by quipping that somebody had to keep him in the fashion to which he was accustomed. Ha ha ha. Ever my hero.

Returning to London and doing the business of 'plus' and 'minus' lists that psychologists always tell us aids decision-making, we thought it all weighed in quite well on the 'plus' side. Most importantly to The Beloved, there was a good solid, daily schedule of Offices (that means, in common parlance, that everybody said their prayers together every day from a good old-fashioned everyday prayer book). And this was informed by good, solid liturgical practice that was lovingly and painstakingly observed and carefully taught. And, of course, there was the small perk of all Oxford, including its lecturers, pubs and Bodleian Library, being on the doorstep.

Our aforementioned friends were happy there and, as

they were expecting their first baby and moving into one of the larger flats, it was not inconceivable that we could move into their very flat. This, we thought, would be quite good for several reasons. The first slightly perverse advantage was that instead of facing into the picturesque college garden, it faced outwards with a stunning and evocative view of the back of the video shop, the roof of Tesco's, the sitting room of two very attractive nurses, verdant thickets of television aerials and the ever-engrossing traffic of the car park. 'Some advantage,' you might say wryly but we were counselled that it does a great deal for the mental health of the ordinand, after a long and trying day in the halls of an eminent theological college, not to have to look at the bloody place as well. The second was that it was at the end of the block of flats and had no one above it. This, too, may seem a little perverse but two years of some two-ton child stomping around or endless gin-soaked Anglican dinner parties above us struck us as something to avoid if at all possible.

And these flats were small – believe that word 'small' in the same way, patient Reader, that you have already believed the word 'steep'. They had originally been built for male, retired members of a fraternity. *Single*, male, retired members of a fraternity. Single MRMs of an F are not thought to take up much room and most particularly they don't take up room when they are cooking or when they are sleeping. Oh, and they're also liable to drown in the bath. So these excellently purpose-built flats had no room to open the fridge door or any cupboard when there were two people in the kitchen, a double bed had to be fitted wall-to-wall like carpet and the bath was only eight inches deep. 'Fussy, eh?' you're thinking to yourself but I saw the prospect of spending two years without having my boobs fully immersed in bathwater as just one more of the small personal sacrifices I was prepared to undergo for the sake of The Beloved. Though I am willing to confess it was not one that had sprung up foremost in my imagination. But you just never know with the dear old C of E, do you? Ingenious really.

So all in all, this particular college had auditioned well. More importantly, they were actually prepared to offer The Beloved a place.

The next college on the list was the one in Cambridge. By now I had finished with the sailor suit and the swimming costume and was in a stunning medieval city in Burgundy doing a spot of Monteverdi. This meant that The Beloved visited Cambridge on his own. The other college near Oxford he decided to give a miss, mainly because of the difficulty of commuting to the world from it without a car. The final upshot of his research was that, while Cambridge had been highly impressive also and had also offered him a place, he felt that the Oxford one was the place he wanted to park his bicycle for the next two years. So it was that all arrangements were put in train, all the spookily formal letters were written and that was that.

Scanning down the list of Important-And-Big-Things-To-Do our conjugal finger now rested on the item that said, 'Buy a house to put all our imminently arriving furniture into.'

This was a bit of a necessity, not only for the convenience of the furniture but because we also needed somewhere to live out of term-time and I could chase my career much more easily from a London base. Also the old-fashioned girl in me says you can never go wrong investing in property. Fact tells us that of course you can (particularly if you are advised by a certain bunch of ecclesiastical commissioners) and that drugs and diamonds are a better bet for making pots of money. But dealing in drugs is not very time-efficient what with all that lurking on street corners and changing your phone number every week and buying impenetrable dark glasses, and I think diamonds look a bit naff with the jeans and Docs that I am invariably wearing, so real estate it was.

Prior to my departure for shores Gallic we had picked out a nice flat not far from where we lived in South London. A bit of an orange and brown disaster decoratively, it was nevertheless pleasant, sunny and recently rewired. Without trying you with the details of the dastardly mortgage-broker who let us down and the heroic bank manager who saved the situation with only seconds to spare, let me inform you that we achieved proud ownership of this flat and the challenge its décor provided.

The Beloved and I then went back to France where I was to spend three months in another Mozart opera and he was to have a bit of a holiday before his first term commenced. He brought all his latest godly reading matter including *Biblical Greek for Absolute Ning-Nongs* and was enjoying himself tremendously splashing around in all this by day and hanging out in the bar in town until my show finished at night.

It was a month before my contract finished and the furniture crested the waves of Dover harbour that he was due to take up residence in the tiny Oxford flat and begin his studies. Rather than sleep on the floor or in the drownproof bath, he bought himself a quick bed and a rejected table and chairs and launched himself into student life at St Stephen's House, most popularly known as 'Staggers'.

The Beloved would consider life in an unfurnished flat, messing around in a lot of books with a lot of praying and studying to do all day, as a slice of Heaven on earth. He would probably consider pursuing such an existence permanently were it not for his great love for me, his partiality for good cider and his unshakeable passion for the music of Jimi Hendrix. So my welcome was joyful when, after a few weeks of his appealingly monastic domicile, I arrived back to join him in Staggers life. This apparently confounded all the green-eyed rumours flying around the other ordinands that The Beloved had invented the existence of a wife in order to get a flat on his own.

Of all the things that I could be accused of, like having a dirty laugh and refusing to wear floral skirts, being fictional was a nice change. It's easy enough to believe that one doesn't exist at all when one is standing in a supermarket queue or trying to attract a waiter's eye at lunchtime on a Friday but to be regarded as a product of imagination or perhaps even unconscious desires is an amusing departure redolent with potential.

My work involved no more touring for a bit and so I flung myself into a painting frenzy in London in an attempt to get the kitchen and bathroom into a state that didn't make food preparation a liability and ablutions an assault. The plan was to get this finished before that Pantechnicon full of widely travelled furniture rolled down the street.

A dear mate, Tim, who professed some experience in these things and uncannily reminds me of my brother in much of his demeanour, offered to assist in wallpaper stripping. So the two of us hired a steamer and set to work. With the limpid strains of late-70s rock bands encouraging our efforts, we sang along, danced, swore and exchanged intimate confidences like you do when you're halfway up a ladder with a boiling steamer in your hand.

Let me give you a glimpse into this scene: The top six layers of wallpaper came off with gratifying ease – a flick with the fingernail at the skirting board, a gentle teasing and then satisfying full lengths could be torn off with a flourish to reveal further brown and orange glories. We found hop-sack-style embossed, olive green and grey florals, a truly frightening aqua-blue geometric and finally made it down to the original lining paper which had been painted in a medicinal shade of calamine lotion pink. This was when we came up against the true ingenuity of the early twentieth-century paint manufacturers. Tim and I decided that there had been a flourishing company whose colourcharts were all the rage at the time. Their advertising spiel went something like this: 'Thinking of decorating your new purpose-built maisonette? Buy Bastard paints and papers. Unborn generations will *never* get them off!' We ended up taking this last layer off in one-inch-square pieces amid a heightened and even more colourful employment of various nouns and adjectives. While Tim remains a friend, he has never since offered any DIY advice.

The immediately necessary work finished, the truck arrived and The Beloved and I reacquainted ourselves with possessions that were but dimly remembered. This was a strange process, like having a time-machine to revisit your own past life. Bookmarks were in the pages where we left them three years previously. Three-year-old telephone messages were still on the notepad. The answering machine had a three-year-old outgoing message on it. All the clothes were suitable to a climate and lifestyle that seemed totally alien now.

Apart from this eeriness, we rejoiced exceedingly in reclining once more in our enormous orthopaedic bed, in having our hi-fi back again and in simply feeling that we were no longer adrift because we had our very own mortgage agreement and we had possessions once more.

Sorting these possessions into meaningful piles and, with the aid of a lovely blue truck which The Beloved nearly took to Birmingham when he missed the Oxford turn-off, we comfortably furnished both our newly acquired London *pied-à-terre* and the Small-But-Perfectly-Formed flat in Staggers. We were now fully girded loin-wise and in a state of readiness to tussle with anything that a Diploma in Theology, and its attendant complications, could chuck at us.

9

CHRISTIANS IN THE LAUNDRY

The question any ordinand's Significant Other resident in a Small-But-Perfectly-Formed college flat will ask themselves is this: 'Does the Christian faith extend as far as the communal laundry?' This is a very different question from, 'Does the ubiquitous benevolence of God extend as far as the communal laundry?' because the answer to that one would have to be a definite 'Yes' or we probably wouldn't have found ourselves living in a theological college.

The answer to the initial question (apart from calming the nameless terror that strikes at the occurrence of the word 'communal') I will not keep you in suspense about. It is, 'Mostly but there are occasional real bad-hair days, if the Christian faith can possibly be said to enjoy such things.'

The rubbish bins, now they're another matter. The same question applied to these would invariably engender, in me at least, a negative response. I encountered here the same inability to find the opening in a large communal (that word again) rubbish bin as one encounters in any suburban recycling centre. People have the energy and good intent to bring the bottles, papers and paraphernalia to the depot but once within proximity of the relevant receptacle a curious and medically interesting condition asserts itself. Their blood sugar level seems unexpectedly to plummet and they come over all woozy and suffer a complete inability to actually put the items *in* the bins. The sorry evidence of this hypoglycaemic malaise, which can strike men and women of any age at any time they are within a recycling depot, one can perceive in the many Sainsbury's bags that one finds cuddling up to the foot of each bin, spilling their contents onto the surrounding paving. The only known cure would seem to be abandoning any bin-filling activity immediately, going straight home and uncorking another bottle of that cheeky little Merlot whose very appeal resulted in the necessity to visit the depot in the first place.

This is a condition that also manifests itself regularly in theological colleges. On any day of the week the large rubbish bins have a similar, small crowd of bags clustering around their bases like toddlers clinging to a mother's shins. In residents' meetings it is always pointed out that 'they' should do something about this, usually the same 'they' that should remember to close the car park gates, volunteer for the garden maintenance rota, sweep the landings or even take the bottles down to the recycling depot.

In general, what I was to learn was that living in a block of flats in a theological college turned out to be much like living in a block of flats anywhere. Mostly people are quite nice and well meaning but the commonality of the Christian faith does not armour them against being fallible and human, much as we would like to believe the television evangelists. And thanks be to God for that, I say. It would be truly scary if it were possible to metamorphose into superbeings simply by confessing to a faith in God. And so boring, too, with no foibles or failings to wrestle with. What's life without a good wrestle, I ask?

Among the varied factors in one's basic and tangential shift in reality that occurs in joining the community of a theological college is the spooky realization that all of your neighbours are in church with you on a Sunday morning.

Another is that all the ordinands' and the college staff's wives are teachers. Every single one of them. Except me, of course. And the high-powered lawyer upstairs. And the nurse. Oh, and the philosophy lecturer. But *apart* from those, they are all teachers. And all their children are called Luke and Sophie.

On my belated arrival, aside from the immediate challenge of running a size 38DD life from a size 32A flat, I found myself abruptly included in many social and domestic situations with all the other clergy wives. And these ladies (at this particular college one would have to search diligently indeed for a clergy husband) had nothing at all in common except for a vague assumption that we shared a set of beliefs and a necessity to be tremendously creative financially for a couple of years.

I should briefly interject, at this point, a word or two about money.

The shared nature of all our conjugal financial arrangements prior to college was changed utterly on arrival. The Beloved not being heir to any discreet private income or a handy barony, it fell to me as wife to earn enough to turn basic grants into living income. Suddenly, my money was our money. For two years.

I don't much mind admitting that it took some heart-searching to be able to accept this with the generosity of spirit that I wanted to. It is perfectly normal for a fiercely independent businesswoman with her own pension plan and shoulderpad collection who exhibits primary Capricornian qualities like myself to feel the occasional, very small niggles of resentment at having someone along for a free ride. Also, unlike the item about the bathwater and my boobs, I had known that this was going to happen right from the start when good old DDO/VIM/VBM had quizzed me. As any loyal and loving wife would, I had staunchly added it to that list of Things-To-Undergo-For-The-Sake-Of-The-Beloved.

And, as with everything in the world, the theory was easy to propound and the practice involved a few more sharp corners, pokey bits and hard work than had been imagined. A bit like Socialism. Or recycling.

But to return to the wives.

Other than the usual daily contact that arises from the fact that one's neighbours are rarely more than six feet away from one in any given direction at any given time, there was a Wives Group. The college principal's wife was kind enough to co-ordinate regular activities, guest speakers, opportunities to eat a lot of things with a high calorific content and general mutually supportive stuff like that. I understand that many prospective clergy wives, when faced with the enormity of the whole ordination thing, find great solace in such company of like sufferers.

Contrarily though, I felt more like an escapologist who was being tied up before being thrust into a very small trunk which would subsequently be bound with massive chains, adorned with padlocks and thrown to the bottom of the sea in the Bermuda Triangle. A bit of sympathy from other escapologists was lovely, but not really going to avail me much once the trunk lid was shut. People who get chained up for a living will make a great to-do, at this point in the act, of writhing and struggling with their captors. This cleverly hides the fact they are flexing all sorts of muscles and filling all sorts of lungs so that their bonds result in being much less restrictive than they look. I spent my energies on the figurative equivalent.

Each time the principal's wife invited me to a wives' gathering I made sure that I wrote very polite notes thanking her for thinking of me and pleading absence or work. This is a discipline that I would warmly encourage any PCW (Prospective Clergy Wife) to master. The Polite Note on nice paper or a pretty card very easily saves unpleasantness in a multiplicity of guises. I found out later at the end of The Beloved's training that, while I had actually attended only two Wives Group gatherings in two years, my brownie points were well up simply because of the Polite Note factor.

So what was I so carefully avoiding?

First, Bible study. I can't stand it. And the thought of doing it in someone's sitting room every week is ghastly to me. To me such personal wrestlings are private and I don't like to do it in company, much the same as I dislike people hearing my vocal warm-ups.

Second, not having any children, it is difficult to discuss them with any command of the subject. After finding out if Luke or Sophie was well and happy and perhaps hearing of the latest of their endearing antics, I would find my conversational impulses drooping. My smile would lose its eagerness and there would be nothing for it but to offer to refill the wine glasses, or fetch more pudding.

Now, it would be cheap and inaccurate of me to suggest that all PCWs (or even fully-fledged CWs) talk about is the Bible and children. That is what the outside world generally imagines we do and I can now reveal to society at large and students of cultural sociology in particular that the tendency is no more marked than in any other group of women. I'm sure it was only my own deep-seated fear of PCW-dom that would cause me to flinch and draw a sharp breath whenever it was suggested I get together with a bunch of them. The Beloved, might I point out, holds a similar reticence about clergy gatherings to this day unless it is sited in a pub or for the purpose of having a good chin-wag about some ambitious colleague with his eyes on a pointy hat.

As it turned out I never actually had to tell any porkies about why I wasn't able to attend Wives Group meetings. Mostly, when I was not away, I was in London working three or four days a week and I would either be staying over in the other flat or else the London–Oxford evening bus services would crest the hill at St Clements too late for me to attend.

The two times I did 'screw my courage to the sticking-place' were for visiting speakers. The first was a bereavement counsellor from the local hospital and a remarkable woman she turned out to be. She was, and I hope still is, one of those saints that, by her example, inspired me to look honestly once more at my own pettiness, accept it honestly and then want very much to do better. Though we wives couldn't quite work out why we were bestowed with the singular advantage of her visit and not the actual ordinands who would have had nothing but benefit from her sensible and wise words.

The second was a return visit from one of last year's PCWs whose Beloved was now in his deaconate. Among the shafts of illumination she cast into the murky depths of our future states I remember, in particular, one story.

Apparently so proud was this Beloved of his newly won clergy garb that he was never out of it. He felt the change his ordination had made in him was ontological and should be seen as such. So his poor wife was living with a man constantly dressed in black who even mowed the lawn in his dog-collar. One Saturday they were due to join their families for a casual picnic and, as this lady assembled cold chicken and quiches, this chap came downstairs in his collar. Not a little sick of this by now she immediately donned her own work uniform, that of a nurse, and refused to take it off until he had changed into shorts. The point was made, the argument carried and he was deterred from such excesses again.

The reason that this anecdote rang true for me was a personally practical one. At that time The Beloved was of firm opinion and accordingly vocal about the probable alienating effects of the traditional all-black clergy uniform. When he was ordained, he said, he was determined to continue to wear his usual jeans and Docs and he had even begun to ask me detailed dressmaking questions about the possibility of altering his usual shirts to fit some sort of understated and easily over-looked clergy collar into them. I had more than an inkling we would go through several versions of this argument in two years, bearing in mind the importance that correct dress held in most people's thinking at this particular college. At this early stage in his training I couldn't see the point of worrying about it and said so.

In common with nuns, some PCWs also harbour innate talents of surprise. Just when you think someone is the most dyed-in-the-wool, Hush Puppy-wearing, self-effacing ordi-nand's wife with a wealth of chutney recipes in the kitchen drawer, they let slip over a custard cream in the Common Room that they are not a teacher at all but a war correspon-dent, or that they have represented England in Olympic shot-put events or that Johnny Rotten is their brother. These PCWs can usually find small and whimsical ways to spring their surprises on you. A jolly good and quite simple one, that works every time, is childbirth in odd places. There is noth-ing guaranteed to arrest the interest of an entire residential theological college like it.

As I have detailed previously, our flat faced outwards into the college car park. And, as I have pointed out before, one of the advantages of this aspect was the superintendence of comings and goings in this area. So it was that one night, well after the witching hour when all good and holy ordinands and their PCWs were well tucked up, that we were awakened by what can only be described as a kerfuffle in the car park. More than that, there was shouting and the occasional scream. Flinging off the wall-to-wall duvet, The Beloved and I poked our heads up under the hem of the curtains like the net-twitching students of our fellow man that we are. It was our imminently parental friends piling into their car. Well, they were trying to pile. While the labouring mother was braced gaspingly against the boot of the car the father was pinging around the car park like the ball in a pinball machine. Fetching a bag from here and putting it there, running round the corner to open the gates, hurtling back to the car to try once more to insert his writhing wife into it, remembering the thermos flask and his gaping front door and narrowly avoiding reasonably certain death as he bounded down the steps once more, three at a time.

The Beloved sagely observed, 'That'll be them having a baby in the car park, then' and we returned to our slumbers in the sure and certain knowledge of what would be the hot gossip over the college cornflakes in the morning.

By the way, I was quite right in my anticipations of living within the sound of bells. I was blessed, although some folk would say otherwise, with a positive concert of them every morning. At six in the morning the nuns over the road would ring their first Angelus – a total of 18 dings. Then at 7.25 the bell for Morning Prayer would roust all somnolent ordinands out of their beds and into the chapel with another. If one listened carefully at 8 a.m., the bell of the college church would bong for five minutes to mark the start of the morning Mass and, if we were lucky and the church up the road was moved to remember Our Lady during its observances, there would be another Angelus by 8.20.

I loved the thought of all those prayers and intentions swinging away on the wind. Nowadays the bells are as much a part of those comfortable, morning household noises as the kettle boiling, the schoolchildren screaming and giggling on their way down the street or The Beloved in the bathroom shouting 'Liar!' at the politicians on the radio.

10

WHAT THE HELL ARE
HERMENEUTICS, ANYWAY?

I continued to keep our conjugal, financial balls in the air
with a heady cocktail of church music, opera and work in
frantic costume departments. As word also got around college
that I plied a nifty needle, I also ended up plying it through
several albs and cottas as The Beloved's fellow ordinands read-
ied their outer as well as inner selves for the big, wide world.

When out in it myself, I was fortunate to still fit shifts
backstage at the National Theatre around the usual Ave Maria
trade, by which I mean singing for weddings and funerals,
which in turn fitted round any opera rehearsals and touring
that I got up to.

Mostly the backstage work was either dressing shock-
ingly human stars of the theatre, those whom I had idolized
all my formative years, or doing their costume maintenance.
If I felt brave enough to confront the canteen menu, I could
even enjoy the thrill of watching them at their lasagne and
chips. The perks to this sort of work were not only the star-
spotting opportunities but also first-hand experience of the
surreal moments that tend to crop up in theatre, particularly
when any sort of historical drama is on the programme. Give
a costume designer a carefully measured inch in historical
drama and you will find their pencils doodling corsets for
impossibly wasp-waisted women, armour so complicated and
heavy that its wearer falls jelly-like into your arms as you

release them from it at the end of the first dress rehearsal and cloaks and trains that comprise yards and yards of prohibitively expensive velvet which are unfailing in sweeping up all the dropped half-sandwiches and cold chips in the canteen during coffee breaks. Roman soldiers bicker over who will have the last finger of the Kit-Kat, Ophelias breastfeed in dressing rooms, Lady Bracknells chainsmoke in corridors, Henry Vs pore over crosswords and Elektras tell the dirtiest jokes you've ever heard.

During a season of *The Crucible* it was part of my instructions to go to the backstage bar during Act Four and purchase one of my gentlemen a pint of beer. This was also the time that the dozen or so prim, young, Puritan virgins, who had just gone hysterical in Act Three, were awaiting the end of the play to take their curtain call. I turned the corner into the bar to find them all, still modestly bonneted and aproned, lolling on the bar stools, screaming at the football replay on the TV, each with a pint in one hand and a cigarette in the other.

My quiet enjoyment of this sort of thing suffered a bruising, though, when I was put to the maintenance on a lavish production of *School for Scandal*. This basically meant the washing and ironing. Washing is fine – fill the lovely big industrial machines and read the paper and drink coffee until they're finished. More of the same for the driers. But then it gets less leisurely. There were 12 gentlemen in this production, each of whom had two shirts, one for Act One and one for Act Two. Each historically accurate shirt had gathered sleeves and lace ruffles and cuffs that had to be starched. And, on Saturdays, there was a matinee as well as an evening performance. And, this being the Royal National Theatre, it was naturally unthinkable that an actor should wear a shirt twice. I will leave the mathematics of those long, hot, steamy and complexion-improving hours to my gentle Reader.

My singing work, however, got ever more interesting as my solo career took reasonably healthy root and I was taken on by an agent whose firm commitment to the welfare of her stable is both commendable and unusual in the industry. I wound up in Wakefield's high-security prison, devising an opera with 30 lifers. (All of them were multiple sex offenders and murderers and they all wrote poetry.) I wound up recording Christmas carols during long and sweaty July afternoons. And I wound up playing a 13-year-old boy ravaged by his own testosterone levels.

This latter was in a production, half-play, half-opera, about the life of Pierre-Augustin Caron de Beaumarchais. I take the liberty of edifying the unknowing with the information that this chap was the diplomat, arms dealer, watchmaker, secret agent and playwright who penned the original anti-establishment plays of *The Barber of Seville* and *The Marriage of Figaro* which have so famously become operas. This remarkable character was seduced by his own sister at the age of 13 and ended up having an incestuous relationship with her for most of his life, three marriages notwithstanding. And I was to be his youthful incarnation until his voice broke and the tenor took over in Act Two.

The seduction scene was reasonably explicit as the other soprano, playing my sister, snogged me and took off a major proportion of my clothing. The end of the scene was a deft removal of my shirt (with my back to the audience, otherwise it would have been just a little more than obvious that I was not actually a boy) and an instantaneous black-out. This sort of thing I am not usually bothered about and neither is The Beloved, having been required to do the same sort of thing in his own thespian career. (The only time he did get a bit upset was watching me, on-stage, going through a wedding ceremony with someone else. Bless his tender heart.)

This gutsy little production toured to Oxford and The

Beloved rounded up a party of people from college to come along to see it one evening. By this time most of The Beloved's colleagues knew me quite well and were not at all surprised or phased by what they saw. All except one German exchange student who, as the other soprano and I were mid-snog, leaned over to The Beloved and whispered, 'How do you feel. . . seeing your wife. . . like this?'

The Beloved shrugged and whispered back, 'How do you think I met her?'

College life in Oxford was bountifully laden with the possibility to acquire new skills beyond perfecting the ability to find the right day of the week in the Alternative Service Book. The Beloved, apart from getting himself appointed as flower lady and consequently on a steep learning curve in the florist's art, was required to do several work experience placements during his two years' training. There were opportunities to shadow hospital chaplains, work in homeless shelters and volunteer in community centres. The Beloved organized himself into a number of positions in an admirably honest addressing of the areas of practical ministry he personally felt to be his weakest.

The first was the straightforward shadowing of our local vicar from South London. This laudable and laid back chap offered The Beloved the chance to tag along with him for the period that he was on a holiday break from college. Then, on the day that this arrangement commenced, he came down with pneumonia and complications and was obliged to leave the running of the parish to his new female curate. This remarkable lady took The Beloved on along with all her other sudden responsibilities and duties and was most wonderfully positive, humorous and supportive. Thus The Beloved was generously involved in the nearest approximation to normal, everyday clergy life in a normal, everyday suburban parish that could have been mustered and he gained a pretty good idea of what it was all like from the altar side of the communion rail.

The second of his placements came via the college. The Beloved became a volunteer in a pre-school playgroup on a reasonably tough estate. This he had deliberately taken on, knowing himself to be inexperienced in dealing with any children that weren't nieces or nephews on the other side of the world. What resulted was a happy rapport with the mothers as he became the only one of the scarce males there to be tolerated in women-only gossip sessions. He also spent long and carefree hours in the sandpit, occasionally accompanied by a toddler or two.

It was The Beloved's third placement that was to have the most lasting effects on his future. An hitherto unexplored interest in the sign language of deaf people was fanned into flame by a visit to the college by an inspiring guest preacher, a woman deacon (now a priest) who is deaf. This quickly led The Beloved to arrange a placement with the Deaf Church and Community Centre in Oxford. In no time it became obvious that he was at a serious disadvantage without the language and that his luxurious handlebar moustache rendered it impossible to lip-read him. He downed two pints and wielded the scissors at the latter problem and enrolled in evening classes at the Deaf Centre for the former.

About the same time, I had become involved with opera workshops with deaf children and was similarly labouring under the disadvantage of constantly having to work through an interpreter. So I decided to accompany The Beloved to the evening classes and we joined a half-dozen crazy, Tuesday students of the wonderful and eternally patient Don. We were warmly encouraged to participate in the life of the Centre and to join the Club on its Friday social whirl, and we loved it all. Not only are we still in touch with friends made there, but I continue to perform signed song and The Beloved has nowadays become an Associate Chaplain to the Deaf Church in London and an advisor in Deaf ministry. From little acorns, etc. And all because of a moustache.

So the time came in this bizarre, hardworking and, shall we say, eternally interesting life to work out where The Beloved was going to go after his college training was completed. All over the country churches designated as training parishes were either waiting with eager hands outstretched to catch their new deacon as he or she tumbled newly ordained from the hands of the bishop, or they were putting away the best altar linens, church plate and delicate old ladies, wearily resigned to another year of potty-training some clumsy maladroit.

Other ordinands at the college had parishes lined up miles in advance and, as the first term of The Beloved's second year was passing, it was getting more than a little worrying that nothing was settled for us. Being sponsored by a central London parish it was known to be most unlikely that there would be any vacancies in the diocese for him to return to. Indeed, in the summer the Bishop of London eventually formally released him, along with 80 per cent of the London-sponsored candidates, to search elsewhere. Cast adrift in this manner, we were not a little uncertain as to what to do for the best and once more lived with a storm cloud of insecurity hovering over the SBPF flat.

But we had reckoned without the labyrinthine ways of the dear old C of E and, more importantly, without the surprising goodness of God.

Now I am not one of those weirdos who believes that, if I pray hard enough for a parking spot on a busy Saturday morning, so important am I to God's greater plan that it will be granted to me and to no one else in the queue. However, if ever there was a fervent prayer directed upwards, it ran along the lines of, 'Please, please, please Lord, don't take me and my singing career and my cosmopolitan tastes and my penchant for Soho fabric shops out of London. I know I am only a blonde and dippy soprano and ultimately superfluous when compared with the likes of Mother Teresa but I'd look upon it as a tremendous favour if The Beloved could practise his ministry within the M25, Lord. Amen.'

A message came from the Vice-Principal one blustery autumn afternoon. The Beloved was to contact him urgently. I hurtled around The Beloved's usual haunts and eventually tracked him down and dragged him to a telephone. The upshot was that there was a rector in North East London who wanted to meet him. We both suffered an immediate onset of the stomach species of butterfly.

Having already been released from the London diocese this seemed like the most miraculous second chance and I was shocked to think that my desperate prayer may have been answered. Rather than build too many cathedrals in the air The Beloved set about reducing my heart-rate to normal and finding out all he could about the parish.

We found out that this rector had something of a stern reputation. Indeed he was said to eat curates for breakfast. In his search for a new one he had already sent a couple back to the kitchen and was now asking to see The Beloved.

The Beloved met The Rector.

The Rector did not eat The Beloved.

The Beloved reported that The Rector was someone he felt he could work well with.

The Beloved reported that there were many strong similarities between their politics and opinions.

The Beloved then reported that he would like to know more.

The Rector asked The Beloved and me to spend a weekend in the parish and meet the elders and holy folk of the congregation.

On the Saturday we were terrifyingly lunched by one of the church wardens and his wife. A superb meal was accessorized by a different wine with every course and finished with the offer of best overproof Jamaican rum. The Beloved did most of the talking as I was too overawed to say much that wasn't fatuous. Afterwards we tottered down the street, taking ourselves for a bit of an explore of the area. We noted the 35 restaurants in Church Street, we noted the West Indian grocers, we noted the Turkish bakeries, we noted the jazz bar, we noted the excellent pubs and we noted the second-hand bookshops. It all looked far too good to be true and we were very frightened.

The next appointment was at teatime with the secretary of the Social Committee and her husband. As the title of the hour only seemed to be nominal, The Beloved accepted a gin and tonic of the size that we later found to be locally known as Rector's Measure. By that stage, though, I was gasping for a cup of tea, said so and was given a lovely tea tray to play with.

That evening we were invited, along with The Rector and his wife and daughters, to a toga party a member of the congregation was having. The Rector drove us there, briefly inserting us into an off-licence on the way. We were most warmly welcomed, though we were toga-less, and had a brilliant time.

The next morning we were in church on our knees with all of these people and it was wonderful – dignified, well-ordered, traditional Anglo-Catholicism without a single sniff of ponce.

From The Rector's lunch table we gazed out over the acre of Rectory garden. Then, before I could grind my heel into his instep, The Beloved took loud issue with a comment of The Rector's and they were off and at it hammer and tongs. The Rector's wife and I looked despairingly at each other. There seemed to be nothing either of us could politely do to arrest the argument so we ignored them and talked about something else. I was mortified and convinced that he had blown it.

We returned to Oxford and tried hard not to hope too much.

One morning, about a week later, The Rector phoned and invited himself to lunch. My butterflies worse than ever, I broke the land speed record over to Tesco's, threw all manner of foodstuffs around the SBPF kitchen and frantically tried to find the dining table under all our books, music and papers. By one o'clock I was ready and the icy calm that usually descends on me at those moments when the stage manager tells me that the leading lady has broken her neck and would I please go on this evening pervaded my very being. From now on I could do nothing more than be honest.

Serious practicalities and approaches and contingencies were discussed over that lunch and at the end The Rector rose and thanked me for my trouble. He then said that he would be pleased to offer The Beloved the place at Stoke Newington, for that is where it was. And then he left as abruptly as he had arrived.

Blinking at each other over the remains of lunch, The Beloved and I first said, 'Whooh' quite a bit and then I cried, of course. Then, as the actuality of what had occurred sank in, we grabbed each other and danced and shouted and hugged in delight all around the spare inches of the SBPF flat. My career was saved from worse than oblivion and The Beloved was to be the curate at St Mary's Stoke Newington. God does indeed work in mysterious ways His wonders to perform.

11

A ROOM WITH A VIEW

So, time it was once more to prepare to haul up our tap-roots, weigh anchor, let out our throttles, strap on our knapsacks and head for the open road. By which I mean that we had to move house again.

I consider myself, in a smallish way, something of an expert on this topic. We had completed this tricky manoeuvre, on average, every 18 months since we first fell into each other's arms. This frequency has bred a familiarity with the whole process which has subsequently led me to formulate a *modus operandi* in a bid to maintain sanity. I take the liberty of passing on 25 handy hints that could streamline the process for any other PCWs (or, indeed, CWs).

1 It seems silly, but make sure you have been endowed with actual sets of keys to the new holy residence and ask those mystifying questions about the window locks, the cellar, the garage, etc. The entire Parish Church Council will have sets of keys too, so there is no need to worry if you mislay yours. Similarly, if you forget the burglar alarm code most of the congregation should be able to remind you and it will probably have been published in past issues of the parish magazine, too.

2 Contact utilities (gas, electricity, telephone) and arrange for final readings to happen the day *before* you move. During your conversations with the ones servicing the

new house make sure you repeat the account number, address and date at least five times and perhaps point out the peril their eternal soul may be in if arrangements go wrong. Also contact your plumber to arrange to disconnect your cooker (if gas) and your washing machine and to do whatever it is they do to immobilize the drum in the latter at the same time.

3 Cultivate a close and meaningful relationship with the new parish's handyman or tame plumber and arrange for him to pop into the new house late on the day you move to reconnect things. Always, always offer him tea and biscuits.

4 Get 'The Beloved Is Revving-Up And We Are Moving – Pray For Us For God's Sake!' cards printed and write all the envelopes for these while he is doing his exams. This is a comforting way to allay sheer panic and gives you the impression that you are doing something useful and necessary.

5 Before you post off all 'For God's Sake!' cards make sure you make a list of whom you have sent them to and remember the whereabouts of the Safe-Place-You-Have-Put-It-In-So-You'll-Know-Where-It-Is. The panic that goes We-Did-Send-One-To-Aunty-Brunnhilde-Didn't-We can then be quickly dealt with.

6 When packing, designate a reserved area or sacred site and into it place a large Necessities Box (see Hint 8), the hoover, mop and the dustpan and brush. With this place another Important Things Box containing all vital papers, files, music, ball-gowns, tiaras, reference books, etc. that you will need during the week *after* you move. This latter is a sanity measure against the sheer enormity of a house you probably hate by now and your entire life missing-in-action in huge stacks of cardboard boxes.

7 Start packing in the rooms least used first. Don't forget

the garage, under the stairs, attics and those high cupboards on the landing that always seem to contain trunks full of old schoolbooks and your father's scout sleeping bag.

8 Into the aforementioned Necessities Box put the following: kettle, tea, coffee, sugar (all removal men have two sugars), milk, tea towel, teaspoons, biscuits (digestives are fine but your discerning removal man prefers gingernuts or Jaffa Cakes), jay-cloths and scourers, bottle of Flash, rubber gloves, enough cups for all involved on the day, gin, tonic, glasses, corkscrew, plasters (someone will invariably graze their knuckles), screwdrivers and a hammer, scissors or a pocket knife, a pen that works, loo roll, soap, your toiletries bag and a large bunch of bananas – trust me, you'll want them.

9 Clean cupboards as you empty them – then it is not such a drama later. This can be quite an enlightening process because the photos for which you have been searching for six months now surface, you'll find where the elusive ant trail was coming from and you'll finally discover where the stopcock is.

10 Methodically eat everything in the freezer so that it is empty to defrost the day before.

11 If you are being really terribly sweet to your successors, fill all nail holes and patch the paintwork. And clean the bathroom – it's its last chance and think what you thought when you first saw it.

12 Among the useful things it is possible to do the day before, you can take your own readings from the gas and electricity meter. Keep them in the Important Things Box. Then, at around 2 p.m., ring and abuse gas and electricity chaps for not turning up. Give them your own readings over the phone and threateningly say that you are keeping them on record. You could mention their

eternal souls again, too. Apply the same treatment to the plumber who will seem to have forgotten you.

13   Don't try to cook anything the night before you move and don't pretend you have no appetite. Go for a curry.

14   Leave another box out for all the bedlinen that's on your bed and add two clean towels. Then on the morning of the *Dies Irae Dies Illa* pack all the bedlinen into this box as soon as you bound from your bed fresh and ready for action – that way it won't get dusty. Put the box in your reserve corner.

15   Eat breakfast. Your mother would say the same. This will probably consist of bananas because you have packed everything else away – See?

16   Following the removal men round with the hoover and hoovering each room as they empty it, sweeping and mopping the kitchen, etc. is a much more creative use of nervous energy than following them drippily around with empty hands saying be careful with that. It also means you will probably not be looking when they drop all the boxes you've marked Fragile and thus keep your stress levels down.

17   Keep everything in your reserve corner until last and then put it nearest the tailgate on the truck or in your own car.

18   Eat a banana.

19   It is interesting to note that, no matter how nippily you make the journey to the new house, the removal men will be patiently waiting there already and will have found the local caff and be gorging themselves on bacon sarnies.

20   Put your Necessities Box in the kitchen, the Important Things Box next to the phone, wherever that may be, and the box of bedlinen in the bedroom.

21   Now MAKE THE BED – don't do anything else first.

Only after this are you allowed to retrieve the kettle, introduce it to its new powerpoint and put it on.

22 Standing decoratively at the front door and directing each box to the correct room means you are on the spot when curious neighbours walk by not peering in for the fifth time and saintly parishioners bring you home-made cake. You can usefully alternate this activity with tea-making and banana-eating for some hours.

23 Do not offer to help the removal men – they have comprehensive insurance for groin injuries and you don't.

24 When every last little thing is in, the removal men have been heartily thanked for such a bonding experience, you have led a round of three cheers and handed over the tip to the gov'ner or driver, sign the papers, say your fond farewells and wave them off. Then lock the house and go to the pub for at least an hour.

25 On your return, carry Beloved over threshold (as refreshment allows), work for as long as you can stand to while remaining conscientiously cheerful and polite in demeanour to your Beloved. When this becomes impossible go for another curry.

Before this diverting and action-packed process could be once more enacted, there were a few small details to clear up first. The first was the all-important redecoration of the palatial new residence.

The Rectory Flat comprises the entire top floor of the enormous Victorian Rectory with its acre of garden, croquet lawn and legendary mulberry tree. This is situated just behind the stunning pile that Sir George and Giles Gilbert Scott had been pleased to erect when asked if they fancied whipping up a parish church in North London. On the doorstep lies the whole of Clissold Park with its ponds, deer and aviary and to the rear both Canary Wharf and St Paul's Cathedral can be seen from the sitting room windows. Were an estate agent to concoct a blurb about it he would have to employ very little hyperbole. 'Rambling' would be an inevitable and undoubted description, as would 'huge' and 'light-filled'. Its proportions are hilariously generous, its views stupendous and its location definitely sought after. A greater contrast to the SBPF flat in Oxford could hardly be imagined.

Practically speaking, although central heating was recently installed after a number of curates had died being eaten by polar bears, and the lovely, plain, innocuous carpet was freshly laid, the paintwork suffered terminally from being variously coloured baby-blue, avocado-green and cack-brown. This I planned to rectify during the second of the small details – the irksome little formality of The Beloved's final exams – before progressing on to the third, the entertaining little trifle of The Beloved's ordination to the deaconate in St Paul's Cathedral.

When The Beloved has something terribly difficult and concentrated to do, he is so well trained in Stanislavsky's Method by his acting school as to actually become his task. Thus he too becomes difficult and concentrated. Well, he certainly did at exam time. Having lived through the gestations and assisted at the births of a novel and a good few stage plays, I recognized signs of labour early and knew in my very vitals that there was only one way to deal with it this time and that was to leave him alone. There was absolutely no point in spending two weeks resident with a humourless disciplinarian with the conversational pizzazz of an Exhaustive Concordance. Far, far better to tenderly, lovingly and self-preservingly get out of his way.

So I went to The Rectory Flat and, for the fortnight that The Beloved struggled to prove his theological worth, I painted. I painted miles and miles and miles of ceilings, skirting boards, windowsills, walls, architraves, doors and Victorian twiddly bits. I slept on the floor until The Rector and his wife realized what I was doing and forced me to borrow their Z-bed and frog-marched me down to their dining-room table for at least one meal a day.

In a burst of common sense I had cleared my diary for about six weeks in order to be on hand for moral support of The Beloved, so I had little or no singing to do. This was also because I knew the paint fumes would render my normally dulcet tones temporarily baritonal and thus not overly useful to me. A bright yellow, Wedgwood blue and barley white rash appeared over my face and forearms with occasional weals of white matt enamel. But I cared for none of these debilitations. I painted morning, noon and night. I painted with total absorption. I painted as though I had no other wish. I painted for The Beloved and for the dear old C of E.

This was actually no imposition. It was early May and the warm sunshine and scents of the blooming garden wafted on the breeze through the flat as I flung open the sky-lights and windows to clear the fumes. Kind parishioners dropped by to welcome me, to wish me well and bring me cake. I ate a lot of bananas. And I was temporarily quite happy to be grubby and unkempt. I had a respite from being smart and impressing anyone. And I was, for the most part, alone.

As a noisy and gregarious being, I do prize solitude. I have always needed sizeable lumps of it, right from early childhood. My wise mother recognized this need and guarded it carefully through my upbringing. My alone times are times of unfettered imagination, speculation, percolation. I allow my usually frenetic thought processes to meander along their own ways free of the usual connection with English syntax and my mouth. Although, now I think of it, the mouth does come into it quite a lot. I find myself happily chatting away to invisible people, articles of furniture, vegetables and, taking a leaf from The Beloved's book, shouting back at the radio. If

I am upset or angry about anything it is usually the fridge that gets the full force of the confrontation I will never allow myself to have in the workplace. By the time I have rehearsed these rants over a few times, altering the script each time to be as biting as possible, my ire is spent and its object safe from harm. I interview myself, recounting formative experiences or theatrical anecdotes for some lifestyle magazine or arts programme. I work out how to organize my life should The Beloved die before I see him again. I read and drink pints of tea. I practise difficult phone calls to prospective employers. I perform show-stopping numbers to the sofa. I design earrings and ballgowns. I look out the window.

One could say that all this is highly self-indulgent and one would be right. But it is by this process all the scraps and niggles and ideas that are whirling around daily settle to mental earth and become either useful or discardable.

The fortnight of this solitary and creative ebullition allowed me to develop a reasonably substantial well of calm with which to fuel the next few weeks. It allowed me time to put my mental and spiritual house in order before I focused all my energies on my next project. Having no single, special gift to give The Beloved to mark this time and occasion, I gave myself. My every thought and action and prayer.

12

BEING IGNORED (2)

We took up residence about three weeks before the date of The Beloved's ordination to the deaconate at St Paul's. The vast amounts of domestic space we now found ourselves cantering around in could be conveyed perhaps by iterating a conversation that took place early the morning after. With no curtains or blinds yet hung, The Beloved and I woke at about five o'clock to the chatter of mating magpies and the clear brightness of early summer sunshine. The bed we had placed beneath two huge skylights and from our recumbent position we could see nothing but pale blue sky and the very tops of the towering lime trees. Small puffs of pink clouds drifted past our newly opened and still blinking eyes. With a sigh of deep satisfaction, The Beloved turned to me and in a sleepily warm voice said, 'I wonder if there is a bus that would go past our loo at this hour of the morning.'

And so we began life in the little slice of Heaven on earth that isn't John Lewis' haberdashery department. We artfully arranged our furniture, we filled the kitchen cupboards with our china and unmatched bits of Tupperware and we introduced the bath ducks to their new abode. Parishioners quietly welcomed us and saw we lacked for nothing but mostly we were allowed the time to organize ourselves and get ready for The Beloved's Big Day.

As far as the actual ordination at St Paul's was concerned, there was obviously little that I had to do. However,

as people who never let an opportunity to organize something go by, we decided to have a bit of a party afterwards for
all with whom we wanted to celebrate the occasion — friends
from All Saints, friends from theatre, friends from Oz, deaf
friends from Oxford as well as the movers and shakers from
St Mary's.

Working this out to be at around 50 people, and taking
into consideration a strong likelihood of sunny weather, I
made the most pleasant acquaintance of Jim and ordered
appropriate quantities of Pimms. Jim ran, and still runs, the
local wine shop and had had a long-standing and highly
fruitful, or should I say 'fruity, full and with a cheeky little
nose of oak' relationship with the church and, in particular,
with The Rector. Jim's ministry to the ministers of the parish
remains of immense value to them, never mind all his other
customers. His was the timely advice to me that The Rector
would not drink Pimms. Indeed, he was rarely seen to drink
anything other than large gins with a sniff of tonic. Grateful
for this direction, I added a bottle of the correct gin to the
list and hoped I would not blunder.

The Beloved next had to be expertly fitted for his
beautiful new cassock. Not quite being free of his theatrical
penchants, he had his heart set on a tailored one rather
than something bought off the rack. Over two weeks the
immaculate gentleman from a well-respected clerical tailor's
establishment tweaked, pinched, chalked, pinned and generally
created wonders and The Beloved left the premises gor-
geously attired in five deep pleats, cape and cuffs and 39
hand-bound buttonholes.

The rest of The Beloved's trousseau had also been
assembled. The wardrobe (apart from the stalwart black 501s
and the Docs) was now full of a row of neat, black poplin
shirts, a trendy, black linen suit (single-breasted), a snappy,
black wool suit (double-breasted) as well as a crisply white

alb, amice and cotta and a cassock-alb made from a frighteningly uncrushable synthetic in a rough weave named 'Oatmeal'. We immediately dubbed it 'the muesli bag'. Not many colours in there, I hear you muse. What happened to the loud rejection of the alienating traditional clergy garb? Well, it happened like this.

On The Rector's fateful visit to us in Oxford he had made it briskly clear that he considered the uniform immutable. There was to be no watering down, no personally inspired adaptation of the priestly look. And there was only the one colour it came in.

'You're either in or you're out of it,' he had stated.

At this rigidity The Beloved later fumed and said 'bloody' quite a few times until, very near fed up with this, I courageously placed myself in the path of one of his finger-waving circuits of the SBPF sitting room. I posited that if this uniform really was so jolly unimportant then he could just jolly well wear it and get on with it. The Beloved, to whom the sagacity of this advice became clear, abruptly ceased his circuit and put the kettle on – ever the pragmatist.

On the morning of the Big Day, a Sunday, we dashed around putting the finishing touches to the party preparations – the artistic flower arrangements complementing the odour of fresh paint, the Pimms (and gin) chilled and the finger buffet in cling-filmed readiness. I had decided to work at All Saints as usual and go on to St Paul's from there. Once more I thought it would be kinder to both of us if we were not actually in the same building for the hours beforehand. So I tore myself from The Beloved's dressing-gowned side with more than a small sense of nervousness and took my stomach full of butterflies off, knowing that the next time I laid eyes on him an irrevocable change would have taken place.

The Beloved was left to himself for a quiet morning's

gearing up. I found out later that he had had an unnerving time of it, too. Just as he was attiring himself in a clerical collar for the very first time and viewing the result in the mirror with a faintly shocked dubiousness, his father rang from Oz. What, I am sure, had its impetus as a wish to make contact on this portentous day ended up as The Beloved defending himself in dismay against a last-ditch stand from his father telling him he was a fool to do it. Most disturbed by this The Beloved returned to his dressing only to be interrupted again by a call from his youngest sister. She had rung with quite the opposite idea and wished him well. The Beloved left the house, never to be plain Mr again, even more acutely aware of the irrevocability of the step he was taking.

His service was not to start until 3.30 but there was a rehearsal late in the morning of who would walk, stand or kneel where, when. About an hour before The Beloved, together with the 24 others Revved up that day, had to swear things (among them solemn allegiance to the Queen), affirm things and avow things. Then everybody was to robe and attempt to process in through a cathedral that was packed shoulder to shoulder.

In all my ardent selflessness, I had taken a small moment or 70 to assemble a natty little outfit for myself for the day. A cleverly tailored linen number in apple green was accessorized with a smart straw hat trimmed to match with a veil and the lace gloves my mother had crocheted when a teenager. I looked the very picture of English niceness and supportive wifedom. Thus attired I met up with Maureen, for whom The Beloved had joyfully worked as a gardener (and who had donned her fascinator in honour of the day), and Andrew, a firm friend from The Beloved's final sombrero-clad days as an actor, and we three ascended the steps of St Paul's in various stages of apprehension. Inside, the vast acreages were rapidly filling but the major perk to hanging out with the Deaf is that they always get to sit at the front in order to see their interpreters properly. With a prearranged agreement to join them, we confidently wrestled our way to the front of the excited and jostling congregation and found all our friends who found us three spare seats. Maureen, a long-standing churchgoer, settled into serene and gracious poise. Andrew had never even been into the cathedral and was much awed but, true to his promise to me, he was being a complete darling of support and never let go of my trembling hand.

At 3.30, with an unnerving noise like a gust of high wind, the congregation rose to its feet. The choir processed in, the College of Minor Canons processed in, the robed clergy processed in, the prebendaries processed in. The first hymn *Come Down, O Love Divine* began and I tried hard to relax sufficiently to unclench my jaw, swallow and sing. Then from the west end of the cathedral, under the shepherding eye of the Bishop and his crook, came the ordinands, each in a Persil-white new surplice. The Beloved, however, had not added one of these to his trousseau, knowing he would have little occasion to wear one at St Mary's. Rather, he had borrowed a sumptuous flowing ivory silk one from a college contemporary. So in the solemn crocodile of easy-care, poly-cotton-clad candidates there walked one striking figure, his hair in a neat plait down his back, the stole I had lovingly and minutely embroidered across his chest, whose robes whispered luxuriously around him. Andrew and I gripped each other and abandoned singing in order to weep with emotion.

'And so the yearning strong,/ With which the soul will long,/ Shall far out pass the power of human telling,' we gulped and wavered.

My power of human telling falters indeed and can only hint of the potency of the rite, the magnitude of the congregation, the visual splendour, the volume of the singing and the overwhelming emotion of seeing my Beloved, not ten feet yet a million miles away from me, at the heart of all this. Once more I gave him up. I felt so hopelessly tiny and I ached with love for the man I was so dramatically divided from.

At the end of the service the newly ordained deacons, shining to their very fingertips, turned to face the congregation and then followed the towering crucifix through them once more. The Beloved wildly looked for me, smiled at me and I knew he had intuited my distress. At this moment the great West Doors of the cathedral were hauled open and the dazzling afternoon sun suddenly flung itself down the entire length of the nave. The deacons walked towards and through the mighty portals flooded in blinding glory. Even Stephen Spielberg couldn't have done it better.

Out on the steps again, earthly mayhem seemed to reign once more. Everyone was trying to reach their particular deacon and the air was alive with congratulations and cheers. There were hundreds of people hugging each other, waving and calling, talking excitedly and cameras whirred and clicked in a great chatter.

I stood on the top step briefly to try to spot The Beloved in all this crowd. Andrew, having momentarily relinquished his grip on my hand, had been swept off in another direction and Maureen was still a good few yards behind me. As I scanned the remarkable scene feeling lost, a very polite hand was placed gently on my wrist. A rather small but superbly dapper man stood by me dressed in a clipped moustache and bow tie and I was quite sure I had never met him before. With tremendous gentility he leaned towards me and said, 'My dear, you have the hat of the afternoon. Congratulations.'

And then, as I uttered surprised and delighted thanks, he disappeared into the crowd. I wish he could know what a kindness he performed that day. The ever-wonderful Beloved apart, he was the one person that day who acknowledged that I had actually achieved anything. The years of financial responsibility and emotional support, the months of preparation, the weeks of painting and organizing, the awful fear of being taken for granted and the hundreds of pounds I was out of pocket just to get The Beloved to these cathedral steps, I felt to be somehow acknowledged in that small courtesy. I was vindicated.

The freeze-frame unfroze and The Beloved waved to me from further down the steps. I shouldered my way down to him to be kissed roundly and hugged tightly in his arms.

13

TRAINER-WHEELS AND
L-PLATES

One of the kinkier aspects of this whole Revving-up business is the delicious and slightly naughty idea that you are sleeping with the curate. I certainly couldn't take my eyes off him for weeks as I got used to his perpetual black garb. The occasional giggle would burst from my lips as I put away clean washing thinking that I knew what colour the curate's pants were today. I knew what he looked like without his glasses on and with his hair out, I knew what shampoo and aftershave he used and I knew what he looked like with no clothes on. Even though, of course, I knew all this for years BR (Before Revving-up), it all had a new frisson about it.

The Beloved, though, took to it all in the proverbial manner of ducks leaping into ponds. He was so happy and comfortable he often forgot how very different things were, at least how different it was that he looked.

One day he was on his bike, pedalling along the road to the supermarket. He was rudely shocked to have a van suddenly pull out of a side street in front of him. Jumping on his brakes, The Beloved closely avoided a nose-dive over the handlebars and the van took off, oblivious to its carelessness. The Beloved recommenced his journey only to have the same van ride him into the gutter not 20 metres down the road. Once more, The Beloved hit the brakes and yelled in fury. But then the van pulled up at traffic lights a little further on. The Beloved also pulled up at the rear of it and proceeded to vent his outrage by pounding repeatedly with his fist on the van's back panel and dubbing the driver with a psychedelic tirade of epithets. It was in the middle of this artistic flow, of which any fellow practitioner of Australian Creative Swearing would have been much in admiration, that the sudden and arresting realization fell on him. Not only was he within the parish on the main shopping street, but he was also within his clerical collar. Mercifully the lights turned green and, with a lightning nimbleness that Titania herself would have envied, he pedalled round into the nearest side street.

The Rector and The Beloved were daily proving to have temperaments so similar that, if they didn't like each other so much, it could have been disastrous making them work together. I have already regaled my patient Reader with several incidents of The Beloved's tendency to say it like it is and to put forward his views in impassioned monologues or rants. What I was not prepared for was the very same character trait in The Rector.

One evening I arrived to meet The Beloved in that remarkable landmark, the Rose and Crown pub that stands next to the church and seems to generously function as the parish meeting room. I had been auditioning for somebody and was looking quite smart, my soprano shoulderpads at their most impressive. As I entered the front bar I clocked the fact that all the regular drinkers were somewhat huddled down one end of the room and The Beloved and The Rector, at a table by themselves, were deep in conversation at the other. I say 'conversation' but in reality it was a little more elevated in temperature than that. I cheerfully approached the table, kissed them both in greeting and sat down, once more registering that the other drinkers were almost saucer-eyed in apprehension and trying valiantly to ignore the fact that they thought the two priests would punch each other very soon and they didn't really want to be called to witness the incident. Also they couldn't work out why the snazzy blonde was kissing them both in such an insouciant manner. The Beloved was just rising out of his chair and poking The Rector in the chest, shouting that it was just not possible to think like that. As the other patrons gasped in fear and desperately stared into the depths of their pints, The Rector grabbed my hands and passionately cried, 'Oh, isn't he wonderful!'

What could I do but agree?

We were also, now that The Beloved was officially on deck, inundated with invitations from kind and welcoming parishioners. The population of this blessed plot has more than the usual quota of musicians, actors, writers, dancers, artists and arty folk of every type per square inch, and we were delighted to find that simply loads of them were churchgoers. The feeling that we had fallen firmly on our feet and that the people that were in the pews were the very people that we would naturally hang out with anyway was a source of joy.

So we were invited to lunch, dinner, drinks and parties all over the parish. I was on my very best behaviour, my naughty word quotient at an all-time low as I tried to get used to The Beloved's new place in the world. I tried hard to be really measured and considered about what I wanted to get involved in and what I did not, to assess when I should raise my guard and when lower it, and to judge between openness and private confidences. It is a delicate challenge to walk the tightrope between being friendly and candid and getting too exclusively involved in personal friendships.

I also did my best to get to know great numbers of people all at once, or at least remember their names. I will admit that, when I couldn't, my histrionic weakness for calling everybody 'darling' came into regular usefulness.

One evening I badly misjudged things, though, and was

abject with remorse for weeks after. We were at dinner with a lovely couple who had really pulled out the stops to present a lovely meal among a tableful of excellent company. Choice wine flowed, delicious food was served and so attentive to my diverting theatrical anecdotes were our generous hosts (despite a couple of Shut-Up-Death-Ray hard stares from The Beloved) that I carried on with a colourful stream of them for quite some time. As I held the floor and the responsive laughter rose in volume, a small pyjama-ed figure crossly beckoned from the door to the lady of the house. This eight-year-old daughter of the house was trying to get some sleep, so please could we keep the noise down. Like naughty teenagers we all froze into silence and I blushed in shame. I had been clumsy once more. I am grateful to say, though, that the incident has not at all impaired our continuing friendship, nor beaten the fondness for a good luvvie story out of us.

The other factor that was a source of daily concern were the number of beggars, drunks and nutters that made their way to the Rectory doors. We like to think, I am sure, that in a country with so very much civilization such people only form a small and not too visual percentage of the population. At once get involved with any of the charitable or caring vocations and the realization that, as Our Lord said so long ago, the poor are always with us, is unavoidable and shocking.

My practised conviction that we should all be doing whatever we can for these people temporarily put aside, I think it is not unfair to state that a significant proportion of those who actually ring at the door of any large Rectory are not entirely genuine. The trick is working out who is to be believed and who is not.

The church kept food parcels to hand out to the needy, but held to a policy of never giving out cash. This well-advertised fact, however, didn't seem to deter some mendicants. The creative invention of their stories was sheer entertainment.

It was, to me, simply remarkable just how many of them had sick relatives in Aberdeen or Belfast, how many nappies the average baby seemed to work their way through in a week, how many Giro cheques failed to arrive before a holiday weekend and how many urine-smelling drunks spent their days gasping for nothing more than a cup of tea. One particular chap who rang our bell two or three times a week never failed to burst into tears when I answered the door, so moved was he by my uncanny resemblance to his dead daughter. Another traveller woman, stunningly clad in leather trousers and large amounts of jewellery became singularly abusive when I wouldn't give her money for dog food. I'm only half-ashamed to admit that the exchange resulted in me advising her to hock the trousers and to sod off.

And the nutters weren't just on our doorstep. Thanks to government policy of the time, every three months would see a new batch of mentally ill people released from the residential care of years into the welcoming arms of 'care in the community'. And a clerical collar or a church tower is an unfailing nutter magnet. One of my favourite characters that haunted the main street was a chap The Beloved and I dubbed Mr Indecisive. This poor man was almost paralysed by his own inability to carry through any action. He always carried a large artist's folio and would walk up and down the pavement, stopping himself every six feet or so to touch his lips, scowl, breathe in, turn and retrace his steps as if he had forgotten something. One afternoon I watched as he caused a traffic jam the entire length of the street as he hovered on the edge of the zebra crossing. He would get halfway across and then turn and go back, only to turn again at the kerb. Another time he held the famous number 73 bus to ransom for nearly five minutes as he repeatedly mounted and got off the rear boarding platform.

Into all this kaleidoscopic existence The Beloved fitted

joyfully, rapidly and easily. I have already mentioned ducks and water but it did seem that, at last, he had found a way in which all parts of him were in balance. He was working energetically, blissfully happy in service and honoured to be made such an intimate part of people's lives.

The regular clientele that drank in the Rose and Crown, and in particular the cabbies, were proud to tell anyone that looked slightly shocked at the sight of a dog-collar in the front bar that the new 'vicar' was all right really – just like a normal bloke. Taking a break from a round of baptismal visits one evening, The Beloved was refreshing himself with a quiet pint and failing to do the crossword, when the collar performed its magnetic act on yet another chap that had always wanted to ask a vicar . . . The Beloved listened to his story with full attention and never turned a hair when he became first heated and then abusive. However he did raise his eyes from the fellow's face at one particularly vicious comment only to see all the cabbies had drifted into a standing semi-circle behind his companion's chair. Their eyes, in turn, were making silent enquiry of The Beloved and then the young landlord, a lightweight boxing champion whose many trophies were displayed above the bar, approached and said loudly, 'There's no trouble here,' looking pointedly at The Beloved's assailant, 'is there, Father?'

And there was a cracking of knuckles and a rolling of shoulders around the group. 'Would you like this . . . sorted, Father?'

Conscious of what such a sorting might entail and of his companion's sudden stillness and pallor, The Beloved thanked them for their concern and assured them that he was quite all right. The man departed with an enviable rapidity.

As we neared our first Christmas in the parish, I was determined to celebrate in a style that we hadn't been able to in the SBPF flat. My thoughts turned to the tree that we now had the space for, to swags of fresh holly and ivy cut from the churchyard, to fairy lights and pickling and baking. An enormous rich fruit cake was prepared, in the long tradition of my family, by allowing regular doses of sherry and brandy to soak into it. Early in our marriage The Beloved described Christmas in my company as 'death by brandy', and this was to be no exception. One day the cooking brandy ran out and as I was about to make do with a measure from the Armagnac bottle, The Beloved arrived home. I was poised with bottle and tablespoon over the cake when he screamed, from the kitchen door, at the sight of what I was about to do. My feeble excuses that it was only a bit and we had run out of the cheap stuff were of no avail. Ordering me not to move an inch he ran back out the door.

He jumped on his bike and dashed down to Jim's. Flinging open the shop door, he breathlessly entreated, 'Jim! Save my marriage!'

On Jim's alarmed enquiry as to what was afoot, The Beloved described the scene he had arrived home to witness. Jim's instant reaction was to grab a half-pint of the cheapest brandy from the shelf behind him and thrust it into The Beloved's hands, 'Good God man! Take that and run! Pay me later.'

Spring came again, as it has a tendency to do and, with it, vast carpets of bluebells in the Rectory garden, the nesting of the kestrels in the church tower and Easter. On Holy Saturday the parish's holy dusters assembled along with the flower ladies, myself among them, to ready the church for the Festival.

My mentor in flower arranging was Dorothy who had taken my raw, instinctive and characteristically extravagant proclivities in this field and honed them with a loving sub-tlety and deftness. Hers was the wisdom that blue flowers never 'read' at a distance, that there should always be an arrangement on the welcome table and that one should never put red and white flowers together in case it reminded any war veterans of blood and bandages. I had first volunteered my help to Dorothy in great secrecy, desperate not to have it known that I was doing such a thing. My innate dread of being detected as any sort of clergy wife stereotype meant that I would sooner have sung *My Way* in a karaoke bar than have been found out to enjoy flower arranging. I have not managed to bring myself to make chutney to this day. At the time Dorothy, slightly bemused, agreed to keep the name of her new assistant a dark mystery. Subsequently, though, she gently encouraged me to come out of the closet about it and I can nowadays admit to flower arranging without any facial tics, shortness of breath or blushing.

What Dorothy actually opened up for me were times of happy and quiet serenity, pottering around an empty and warmly silent church with armfuls of fragrant blooms and wet greenery and buckets of water. Working with living colour and form in shafts of light from the stained glass windows was, and continues to be, a source of quiet enchantment to me. And I have recently been delighted to find out that the patron saint of all florists is none other than St Dorothy.

So on that Holy Saturday the church bustled with much polishing, hoovering, candle trimming, hymn book counting and much charging about and shouting at each other by The Beloved and The Rector. And much unabashed flower arranging. However, by mid-morning, disaster struck and not a single clean cloth or duster could be found. The Beloved raced over to where Dorothy and I were knee-deep in gypsophila, gerboras and greenery and asked if he could raid the rag bag in our airing cupboard upstairs. Distractedly agreeing, I only realized the seriousness of this after The Beloved had returned with the new supplies. A great shriek of concerted laughter came from the nave of the church where I hurried to find The Beloved twirling things over his head before throwing them to the waiting hands of the holy dusters. Then I remembered that I had recently bought him a dozen new pairs of underpants and relegated the tatty old ones to said rag bag. Tom Jones had a serious rival that morning and several of the volunteers later confided to me that they had never known anything to polish quite as effectively as the curate's pants, particularly the red ones.

14

CHEWING THE CARPET

I now know that, should I ever suddenly mislay all the abilities that I presently employ to keep body, soul and sanity in the one place at the same time, I could always get a job as a professional wedding co-ordinator. Not that I've had any firm offers, you understand, but the organizational talents I was required to bring into play for The Beloved's ordination to the priesthood and his first Mass, I think, more than qualify me for the position. My CV would have to say no more than, 'Has pulled off one Priestly Ordination with Bishop and one Choral High Mass with Lunch', and I would be straight in at the top.

It may not sound much, I suppose – a simple matter of remembering not to swear in front of the VIM/VBM/DDO who was now the Area Bishop, making sure The Beloved's alb is washed and ironed, there are a few sandwiches around and getting the urns to boil in time, you'd say. Well, all I can say is 'tosh' to that.

To anyone a little fuzzy about what it all means and why it is so important, I will take a quick detour to explain. A newly ordained and fully fledged priest saying his or her first Mass is the first time they perform the most important function of their Vocation. As we of the church gather for the Eucharist in enactment of the Last Supper, we step into the apostles' shoes and the priest becomes for us as Christ was to them. Through the priest's actions Christ is made present to us in the bread and wine. It is one of the great sacraments along with Baptism, Marriage and the Last Rites. It is also an excellent excuse for a party.

As with any wedding, the planning started months in advance. And, as with any wedding, so did the arguments. Well, not so much arguments but a series of small creative tussles. It began when I addressed the fatal words, 'What would you like to happen?' to The Beloved. Foolish really and I should have known better but there are some lessons that take a lot of learning. In response to this ill-advised enquiry The Beloved replied that he didn't want a fuss and would say his first Mass at the normal 8.00 a.m. weekday service.

I'll just allow a moment for the full insanity and fatuousness of that idea to sink in.

He had spent a glorious year being trained in a parish of exciting and loving people who were terribly proud of him. His mother and eldest sister were flying from Australia. His father even began speaking to him. The highly proficient Social Committee, justly renowned for their fabulous parish lunches, were poised on the starting blocks. Half the professional choral singers in London had declared themselves on stand-by. The formidable servers team from All Saints had even offered their attendance. And he wanted to mumble away at some ungodly hour on a Wednesday morning when anyone potty enough to be awake would certainly not be trotting down to church for a quick 20-minute said Eucharist. I present that his wife was spluttering in disbelief at the notion and appalled at the idea of such a lost opportunity.

His wife, mercifully, was also vindicated when The Rector pointed out what a slap in the face to all of the above a hole-in-the-corner affair would be. So we dealt with that one swiftly and deftly.

The Beloved, to his credit, then flung humility to the

winds and swung to the opposite extreme (which, of course, was precisely where we all wanted him). Wholeheartedly he started planning a lavish bash, dripping with music, vestments, incense, acolytes, ceremony and pomp. We were going the whole hog out of the sheer joy of celebrating and because we could.

Having had his ideas of a simple and quiet first Mass blown out of the water by all around him who felt a party coming on, The Beloved now felt justified in indulging a few of his theatrical tendencies. And these, metaphorically, had a lovely wide stage with plenty of wing-space, an orchestra pit and a fly-tower to play in. There were two acts to this drama. Act One would be on the Wednesday evening when the Bishop popped round to ordain him priest. Act Two with Grand Finale would be on the Saturday at midday when The Beloved presided at his first Mass, heading a cast of thousands, after which would be a Garden Party to rival our Sovereign Lady's.

The careful balance that it was important to strike between all the loving support and participation of the regular parishioners and that of family, friends and colleagues outside the parish was something that took a large amount of discussion. This discussion was ably furthered, and even somewhat inspired, by a variety of refreshments. Not rarely did we recall the valuable advice of The Beloved's Old Testament tutor who said, 'Gin and aspirin, dear boy! It can all be achieved with gin and aspirin.' However, we did take the liberty of varying this cocktail occasionally to include Irish whiskey, cider, several sorts of Vino Desperado and Nurofen.

To begin with, the regular liturgy at St Mary's is pretty special any day of the year. The task was to find the windows in this highly pleasing framework for the offerings of all the friends dying to sing, the family planning to cross the globe and the colleagues aching to preach. And then there was the ever-important question of what to wear.

We came up with this:

On the Wednesday evening we would all pile into the church as the Bishop laid hands on The Beloved, charged him with several duties, heard him make various declarations, anointed and vested him. This done, we would segue into a High Mass. Bishop to preside and preach. Rector to deacon. Gold vestments. Fr Chris to interpret for the Deaf. Church elder, Mercy, to read. Good friend, Martin, to sing litany. Wife, good friend Corinne and resident early music specialist John to render *Cantate Domino* by Monteverdi.

The following Saturday at midday we would similarly pile into church again. The then Director of Music at St Mary's (a formidable musician who needed but scant encouragement to indulge his fine sense of occasion) had written choral harmonizations to every congregational response in Merbecke, a particularly overwhelming and glorious three-part descant to *Be Thou My Vision* and an organ voluntary as introduction to the recessional hymn *We Stand for God* (a tub-thumper from The Beloved's school days in Oz). This would be scattered among *St Patrick's Breastplate* as processional, the *Messe Solennelle* by Langlais and the anthem *Welcome Sweet and Sacred Feast* by Finzi. This lot was to be rendered by the 25 professional voices of the *Clemens Non Papa Singers* all agog to sing a tremendous amount for the sake of The Beloved and an excellent lunch. Fr Simon, The Beloved's first spiritual director, to preach. Sister to read. Rector to deacon. Full serving team. Red vestments (as is proper to a Mass for the Holy Spirit). Mother to accept flowers. Social Committee to provide lunch for 200.

Anyone who has staged a production of Wagner's *Ring Cycle* lately will appreciate just how much had to be done to bring this off. Anyone who hasn't would do well to be highly impressed that we did.

Two weeks before the Feast of St Peter the Apostle, the

day of The Beloved's ordination, letters were shooting out of The Rectory Flat and phone calls flooding in as rehearsals were organized, a car was hired, music was copied and compiled, flowers were ordered, vestments were borrowed, orders of service finalized and printed, every bed we could find was made up with clean linen and the bathroom was cleaned. As you have already learned, my tendency in times of stress is to whip myself up into a housework frenzy and this joyful time was no exception. There I was going round the bathroom taps with descaler and an old toothbrush, retrieving the hairy monsters from the plugholes, defrosting the fridge, vacuuming the hectares of Rectory Flat carpet to within an inch of their lives and even polishing the brass candlesticks given to me by my mother-in-law to a blinding lustre against her impending arrival.

As a rule The Beloved does not feel the same need for domestic expiation of tension. His methods are much more level-headed and infuriating. He either vents his frustrations in short bursts of stomping around the house, shouting and saying 'bloody' a lot, or else he goes very quiet and slips away. In this particular action-packed build-up to Petertide he did the latter.

He went away to Oxfordshire on retreat – the laudable and proper thing to do in preparation for such a solemn and momentous occasion. And also the wisest thing to do. The prospects for a bit of quiet introspection when his loving wife is at full organizational steam are, to be honest, scant.

The Beloved holds in high regard and loving esteem all nuns. One should never underestimate a nun. One should never put anything past a nun. Nuns are remarkable, surprising and important people. Being taught to play football at the age of five-and-a-half by Sister Julian in full habit and starched wimple is but one formative experience that has left The Beloved with admiration for all her sisters and an unshakeable impression that they are capable of very nearly anything. So it was to nuns that he turned for the space and quiet reflection he needed before the explosive celebrations.

In our hired car I drove him out to Freeland beyond Oxford. The early summer was a glory over the countryside and the birdsong carolled of excitement and cheerfulness. We pootled up and down country roads until we nosed into the storybook village with its picturesque pub next to the old stone retreat house. Pushing open the huge gothic-arched door, we nearly tripped over the table with fresh farm eggs and nun-made lemon curd for sale and were greeted by the retreat house cat and the Guest Sister. The whole place had the warm, quietly ringing calm and silence that only happens in places of deep prayer and scrupulous cleanliness. The Beloved had already started to glow in the way he always does when he's been on retreat. I left him to it.

Yet another letting go – as painful as ever. I can't stay with him to share these times, often as he asks me to. They wouldn't be his retreat if I did. I am acutely aware of The Beloved's needs and intentions at these times and of the inevitability that my proximity would throw it all out of kilter. And I like to think that I am blessed with a reasonably good sense of timing, if nothing else.

Knowing I wouldn't hear from The Beloved for a week, I turned myself into the person that lives without him and headed back to London.

Right!

In three days' time The Beloved's mother, Norma, and his eldest sister, Marea, would be arriving from Oz, kicking off the sequence of events that was bound to leave most of us gasping. I had to set up and man (or more accurately woman) Operation Ordination Headquarters. There was nothing that I couldn't organize now. I was amazing. I was nigh on super-human. I was very nearly at full steam – an energy level that frequently both alarms and impresses all who know me at all well. Only rigid self-control would prevent me from jumping into phone boxes and emerging in red underpants.

In fact, the worst of the organization was complete and all I really had to do was direct the traffic, keep the kettle boiled and the gin cold.

Flights from Oz only ever seem to arrive at rather ungodly hours of the morning. Or it may be that our visitors only take the flights that heave into Heathrow somewhere between 5.30 a.m. and 6.30 a.m. No one is at their best at such an hour and those who manage to look perky, pressed, washed and ready for a four-hour conference call are just weird in my book. I try not to meet their eyes as they skip through the arrivals door, nervous that I will see something there that should be in a Stephen King novel, or that I will be killed in some international Wink Murder game. This early arrival is also difficult to meet if you are, like us, people committed enough to ecological issues to refuse to own a car. The answer to this and all the other logistical posers this Petertide was to treat ourselves to the aforementioned hired one.

I was quite clean and vertical, but very little more, as I stood waiting in the arrivals hall at 5.45 a.m. It was only then that I realized that I had not seen either Norma or Marea for nearly six years, and I immediately became terrified that I would not recognize them.

After agonized minutes of inspecting all the arrivals closely and even looking into the scary eyes of the perky ones, the instantly recognizable figures of a crumpled Norma and Marea finally were led through the sliding doors by their luggage and we all fell into each other's arms.

The most important thing to do with visitors that arrive from Oz at this hour is to KEEP THEM AWAKE. Wash them, take them for gentle walks but do not let them lie down, even for a moment. Let them telephone the rest of the loved ones in Oz to assure them that they have survived the flight, have not once been hijacked and their luggage is not in Alaska but right here in the guest room. Gently remind them that calls to Oz are far from cheap and it's nearly the middle of the night there. Ply them with tea or coffee and regular, light nourishing meals and believe them when they say they couldn't eat a thing but once let them get anywhere near horizontal and you have lost them. They will fall unconscious for the rest of the day and spend the rest of their visit wrestling with the monster Jet Lag. Americans complain about this difficulty a lot, but I can assure you that no one gets jet lag like Aussies. Let's face it, they come from the other side of the world, spending nearly 30 hours in confined, dehydrating spaces. It's an experience that is bound to have debilitating effects that have to be carefully and rigidly managed. So I say again, if you love them, keep them awake.

You can finally relax this iron regime after eight o'clock in the evening. It is also important to remember that any vital survival information you may proffer on this first day will not actually enter anyone's databank.

Norma and Marea were accordingly washed, fed and watered and gently propped upright on the sofa. We chatted over family news, smiled over photographs and finally decided to take a walk along Church Street. While not wanting to alarm either of them unduly, I had impressed upon them that it was probably better for them not to answer the door. The number of mendicant tramps, penitent drunks and nutters that knock at the door of a landmark Rectory behind a land-mark church, as we know, are not few. I felt it was more than could be expected of my exhausted visitors than to ask them to deal with them, never mind any of the other regular traffic of a clergy house. I related a few humorous doorstep incidents of the past months and told of a couple of the more outlandish nutters. They laughed and swallowed the stories with the pinch of salt that anyone with a theatrical in the family always has to hand.

We strolled out along the street. The sun shone, birds sang and the number 73 buses looked their jolliest red. Pointing out the wartime camouflage paint still on the Town Hall, the seventeenth-century houses still standing and Mr Indecisive's crossing, we came to the spot where a housing co-operative was in the process of building a bunch of new dwellings. Piles of sand and building paraphernalia lay around and boards covered holes in the pavement. A somewhat wild-eyed woman coming towards us picked up a handy brick and, screaming violent abuse, threatened to brain me with it.

To this day, I am not aware of what had upset her. I only know it wasn't me and, consequently, I was much more cross than frightened. Without being conscious of any proper *modus operandi*, I began circling around her, my main thought being to defray her aim from Norma and Marea. And I shouted too – even louder and, may I say, in a much better trained voice. I shouted, as to a recalcitrant schoolchild, 'Don't be so bloody stupid! Put the brick down and stop it at once!'

A few repetitions of these handy phrases seemed to impress upon her that she had certainly met her match as far as volume and stubbornness were concerned. Marea had briskly got Norma to a safe distance and herself in position to disarm the woman from behind. She was ready to spring, and I had reached a stentorian volume, when the woman, in the most glowering manner she could, threw the brick into a pile of sand and marched off. The three of us looked at each other in some bemusement, then shrugged and agreed it was probably time to go to the teashop. The moral is never underestimate the women in our family. Or nutters. Or nuns, of course.

A week later, having retrieved a now glowing Beloved from Oxfordshire, the three of us women found ourselves in the front pew in church. The Bishop was filling the vast acoustic with his sonorous tones and The Beloved lay prostrate in front of him, in his own words, 'chewing the carpet'. We were in various modes of tension. Norma, having rarely been inside an Anglican church before, was agog at ceremony and vestments she hadn't seen since before Vatican II. Marea was awed by the proximity of such an impressive figure of a Bishop. I was simply, at every moment, on the verge of weeping with pride in my Beloved.

I will relate three wonderful moments of that evening.

The first was before the service, when Norma quietly gave The Beloved a small psalter that his father had sent. This gesture alone, after all the arguments and hurt over his perceived apostasy, was powerful but inside the front cover his father had written a passage from Corinthians: 'except you utter by the tongue plain speech, how shall it be known what is said? For you shall be speaking into the air.'

That was when The Beloved cried.

The second was when, as part of the ordination, The Beloved was to be presented with a Bible. Now, the family in Oz had sent, as their gift, a beautiful leather-bound Authorized Version with all their names inscribed inside. The Bishop, much in admiration of the lovely gift, had agreed at the last minute to present this particular Bible to The Beloved during the service. As he placed rich red leather and gold writing into The Beloved's hands, we felt that the other side of the world was no distance at all. That was when Marea cried.

The third was during the service when, the actual ordination over, The Bishop turned The shining Beloved to face the expectant congregation and asked them to welcome their new priest. A jubilant thunder of cheers and applause crashed through the church. That was when we all cried. The Bishop picked Norma up off her feet and gave her a resounding kiss on the lips and the rest of us took nearly 20 minutes to exchange the Peace.

A strange effect on me of that evening, that I had never anticipated, was that I couldn't stop looking at The Beloved's hands. When The Bishop had anointed him he had marked both his hands as well as his head. The power of that act seemed to sear through each palm. I was only a few feet away and I had seen the shock run through The Beloved's body like electricity. For weeks afterwards I found my eyes power-fully drawn to his hands, even engaged in the most everyday tasks. And I felt almost shy to be touched by them.

His first Mass was an equally emotionally charged cele-bration. Hundreds of loving and excited faces glowed around that altar. I had realized early on that I would be in no state to be sensible about much and so had asked another good friend to conduct the choir. The magnitude of sound that Stephen harnessed from the assembled friends in the choir stalls was a true glory and I dare to say that even Langlais would have been stunned at the seismic force of the opening bars of the Sanctus. It almost outdid Mr Hitler's best efforts on the roof.

The Beloved was, as we could all confidently expect, absolutely wonderful. He did absolutely everything right. Well, nearly absolutely everything. Well, it's an awful lot to expect one fresh and crispy new priest to get it right all at once. And, in fact, he did nothing worse than the tiny blunders of skipping the Benedictus and completely forget-ting the words of the Creed. And anyway, neither his preacher or his deacon, The Rector, could remember them either, so it can't be that heinous a sin. Eventually the sub-deacon, having furiously and with great poise scrabbled through the books in one of the clergy stalls, found a copy and we could go on. The Beloved's best friend Jeremy had broken his glasses during his first Mass and we had heard horror stories of acolytes tripping over, pints of communion wine everywhere and burning altar linens from other priestly colleagues. I am informed that our Lord is an indulgent God who accepts all our best efforts in the spirit in which they are intended. I am also personally confident that He has a highly refined sense of humour. Watching humanity must be not unlike us watching small children enacting a nativity play. There they are, all got up in a variety of tablecloths, curtains, teatowels, wire coathangers and tinsel, earnestly singing, being a sheep, believing they should have been Mary and wanting to go to the toilet. How could one not laugh while swallowing the lump in one's throat?

At the end of the service, having surpassed even himself in musical grandeur, David at the organ launched into the postlude. Even this was specially planned. Taking pride in indulging his passion for new music, The Beloved had commissioned one of our composer friends, Julian, to arrange a favourite tune for the organ. Julian had spent loving hours working on this. The premiere was eagerly anticipated. David had researched styles and influences in his rehearsals. New ground was about to be broken. And so a little bit of history was created as the combined efforts of The Beloved, Julian and David sent *Purple Haze* by Jimi Hendrix echoing round the church.

In a corner of the Rectory garden, later that glorious, happy summer afternoon, I found an unoccupied chair and took the chance for a small breather. Norma and Marea had been treated with all the honour accorded to visiting royalty. The Beloved had been hugged and kissed into a state of near stupefaction. Speeches had been cheered and applauded. The vast and sumptuous repast had been consumed. The choir had just about drunk us dry and were now attempting a rematch in the Rose and Crown. There were children chasing through the garden beds, a couple of friends snogging under the mulberry tree, a major gossip session going on over the washing-up and a game of boules in passionate process. To deserve all this richness, as Julie Andrews sings in *The Sound of Music*, 'somewhere in my youth or childhood I must have done something good'.

And, for a moment, I sat still.

God give us rain when we expect sun.
Give us music when we expect trouble.
Give us tears when we expect breakfast.
Give us dreams when we expect a storm.
Give us a stray dog when we expect congratulations.
God play with us, turn us sideways and around.
Amen.

(From *A Common Prayer* by Michael Leunig, Collins Dove, a division of HarperCollins Publishers (Australia) Pty Ltd, 1990. Used with permission.)